About Test Prep Connection:

Welcome to RBP Books' Connection series. You [...] for your child or your students. Rainbow Bridge [...] mer educational materials for the past ten years. Now [...] ed to year-round educational support materials for c[...]  .terials 1 sum- xpand-

Their newest release, *Test Prep Connection,* provides students with focused practice in taking reading, language arts, and mathematics tests. *Test Prep Connection* is designed to help reinforce and develop standardized test-taking skills and skills based on NCTM (National Council of Teachers of Mathematics) and NCTE (National Council of Teachers of English) standards for second-grade students.

Anyone who understands children and the nature of learning would agree that a standardized test cannot fully measure a child's understanding, a teacher's effectiveness, or a school's performance. A standardized test is merely a measure of a child's or a group of children's performance on a given day and under certain circumstances. However, since schools and school systems are being held accountable for student performance, some means of providing objective information is essential. Thus, standardized tests have become a popular tool for measuring achievement.

The purpose of this book is to help students improve performance on standardized tests. The authors have carefully targeted topics known to give students the most difficulty: for instance, drawing inferences, estimation, and problem solving.

The content of *Test Prep Connection Grade 2* is grade-specific and based on recent editions of the following standardized achievement tests:

- ✔ California Achievement Tests (CAT)
- ✔ Comprehensive Tests of Basic Skills (CTBS)
- ✔ Iowa Tests of Basic Skills (ITBS)
- ✔ Metropolitan Achievement Tests (MAT)
- ✔ Standard Achievement Tests (SAT)

As you use *Test Prep Connection Grade 2,* you will find a table of contents that will guide you through the skills covered and an answer key that allows you to follow your child's progress. A sample answer sheet is also included, which you can copy and use to familiarize your child with the format of standardized achievement tests and provide practice in filling in answers.

Dear Parents and Educators,

Thank you for choosing this Rainbow Bridge Publishing educational product for your children and students. We take great pride in being involved with your educational experience. Some people say that math will always be math, and reading will always be reading, but we do not share that opinion. Reading, math, spelling, writing, geography, science, history, and other academic subjects will always be some of life's most fulfilling adventures and should be taught with passion both at home and in the classroom. Because of this, we at Rainbow Bridge Publishing try to capture and encourage this passion in every product we create.

It is our mission to provide materials that not only explain, but also amaze; not only review, but also encourage; not only guide, but also lead. Every product contains clear, concise instructions; appropriate sample work; and engaging, grade-appropriate content created by classroom teachers and writers that is based on national standards to support your best educational efforts. We hope you enjoy our company's products as you embark on your adventure. Thank you for bringing us along.

Sincerely,

George Starks
Associate Publisher
Rainbow Bridge Publishing

Test Prep Connection™ • Grade 2
Written by Alison Lawson

© 2004 Rainbow Bridge Publishing. All rights reserved.

Permission to Reproduce

Rainbow Bridge Publishing grants the right to the individual purchaser to reproduce the student activity materials in this book for noncommercial individual or classroom use only. Reproduction for an entire school or school system is strictly prohibited. No part of this publication may be reproduced for storage in a retrieval system or transmitted in any form or by any means, electronic, mechanical, recording, or otherwise, without the prior written permission of the publisher.
For information, call or write: Rainbow Bridge Publishing, Inc. • PO Box 571470 • Salt Lake City, Utah 84157-1470 • Tel: (801) 268-8887

Publisher
Scott G. Van Leeuwen

Associate Publisher
George Starks

Series Creator
Michele Van Leeuwen

Illustrations
Amanda Sorensen

Visual Design and Layout
Andy Carlson, Robyn Funk, Zachary Johnson

Editorial Director
Paul Rawlins

Copy Editors and Proofreaders
Kim Carlson, Lori Davis, Jeanna Mason

Please visit our website at
www.summerbridgeactivities.com
for supplements, additions, and corrections to this book.

First Edition 2004

For orders call 1-800-598-1441
Discounts available for quantity orders

ISBN: 1-932210-85-7

PRINTED IN THE UNITED STATES OF AMERICA
10 9 8 7 6 5 4 3 2 1

Test Prep Connection — Grade 2
Table of Contents

Letter to Parents 4
Test-Taking Tips 5

Reading
Word Analysis
Word Sounds 7
Word Recognition 10
Word Skills 12
Compound Words 14
Contractions 17
Root Words, Prefixes, and Suffixes . . . 20
Sample Test 24

Vocabulary
Picture Vocabulary 28
Vocabulary Skills 30
Synonyms 32
Antonyms 34
Homonyms 36
Multi-Meaning Words 37
Words in Context 38
Sample Test 40

Comprehension
Picture Comprehension 44
Critical Reading 46
Story Comprehension 48
Sample Test 51

Language
Mechanics
Capitalization 55
Punctuation 58
Capitalization and Punctuation 61
Spelling 64
Sample Test 70

Expression
Usage 74
Sentences 78
Paragraphs 82
Study Skills 86
Sample Test 88

Math
Concepts
Number Concepts 91
Patterns 94
Place Value 96
Properties 100
Sample Test 103

Computation
Addition 106
Subtraction 109
Addition and Subtraction 112
Multiplication 115
Division 117
Sample Test 118

Applications
Time 122
Money 125
Estimation 127
Fractions 130
Measurement 132
Geometry 134
Problem Solving 136
Sample Test 139

Appendix
Sample Answer Sheet 153
Answer Pages 154

To Parents

Dear Parent:

Your school will be giving various tests throughout the year to measure your child's performance. The questions on these tests will relate to information your child is learning in school. Some of the tests may be national standardized tests, while other tests will be specific to your state. Whatever test is administered, the results are used to measure student achievement.

Often, even though children know the subject matter, they may not do well on the tests. Test anxiety is frequently created by a fear of the unknown: What questions will be asked? What happens if my score is low? In addition, the test environment for a standardized test can be quite different from the normal test-taking routine, since children are given a limited length of time to complete each section of the test.

The purpose of *Test Prep Connection Grade 2* is to help you as a parent work with your child in order to decrease his/her test anxiety. The book contains practice test exercises that will familiarize your child with test directions, format, and simulated content. A sample answer sheet is included to give your child practice in filling in answers on a separate sheet.

As a parent, you can help your child perform on the test as well as he/she is able. Here are some suggestions:

- Look over the practice exercises that your child has completed, and review troublesome content.

- Practice using a timer with your child to start and end an exercise.

- Emphasize the following test-taking tips with your child:

    - Read all the directions carefully.

    - Look over the whole test section before you begin.

    - Read all the answer choices before you choose one.

    - Do not spend too much time on any one question.

    - Use all the time you are given. Look back over your answers.

    - Stay calm and focus on the test.

- Be sure your child gets a good night's sleep the night before the test.

- On the morning of the test, allow plenty of time for a good breakfast.

By spending time with your child practicing these sample exercises, you will show your child that you are interested in how he/she performs on the standardized achievement tests. Good luck!

Sincerely,

Alison Lawson
Author of *Test Prep Connection Grade 2*

Test-Taking Tips

- It is important to do your best on standardized tests because the test results are used to compare your performance with other students in your school and to compare your school with other schools.

- Studying for standardized tests may seem difficult, but the things you learn in school will help you do well on these tests. One of the best ways to prepare for standardized tests is to work hard all year and learn as much as you can.

- Be sure to have a good eraser and an extra, sharpened #2 pencil.

- Always read all of the directions carefully before you begin. Listen to the instructions that your teacher gives you.

- Pay attention to the STOP and GO ON signs at the bottom of each page.

- Read each item carefully. Then read all the answer choices even though you may think you know the answer.

- If you do not find the answer that you think is correct, review the answer choices. If you are sure that the correct answer is not given, fill in the bubble for "Not given."

- If you do not know the correct answer, eliminate the answers you know are wrong. Then, choose the best answer from the choices that remain.

- Use scratch paper to work your answers if your teacher tells you it is permitted.

- **Be sure to mark your answers correctly.**

    - Fill in the answer space completely.   ○ ● ○ **Correct**
    - Mark only one answer.   ● ● ○ **Wrong**
    - Make your mark dark and solid.   ○ ○ ⊘ **Wrong**

Test-Taking Tips

Sometimes it is necessary to guess on a standardized test. Some questions may ask about content that has not been included in your textbook. Other questions may be difficult, or you may not remember the answer. On many standardized tests, if you do not answer a question it will be scored as a wrong answer. When that is the case, it is important to answer each question.

If you have to guess, here are some suggestions for making the best guess you possibly can on a multiple choice test. (Remember, these are only suggestions. They will not always help you choose the correct answer.)

1. Select an answer that matches the grammar in the question.
   For example, in the question below, answer B is wrong because the grammar is incorrect.
   Question:
   Second graders who want to score high on achievement tests _____

   Ⓐ should never do their homework.

   Ⓑ has not gotten a good night's sleep.

   Ⓒ should always do their homework.

   Ⓓ pay close attention to the teacher's directions.

2. Select answers that contain words such as *many, often, some, usually,* and *frequently*.

3. Do not select answers that contain words such as *all, always, every, never,* and *none*.

4. If there are answers that say about the same thing, do not select either answer.

5. If there are answers that are opposite from each other, select one of these answers.

6. Select the answer "All of the above" or "Not given."

7. Select the longest answer.

8. Select an answer toward the middle.

| Name | Date |

Word Sounds

Directions: Read each item. Answer each question carefully.

Examples:
A. What word begins with the same sound as <u>chair</u>?
 Ⓐ share Ⓑ play
 ● chop Ⓓ which

B. What word has the same vowel sound as <u>table</u>?
 Ⓐ crumb ● anchor
 Ⓒ cat Ⓓ tack

 Remember, each question will ask something different. Make sure you answer what each question asks.

Practice

1. What word begins with the same sound as <u>blaze</u>?
 Ⓐ black
 Ⓑ flower
 Ⓒ flight
 Ⓓ gleam

2. What word begins with the same sound as <u>trick</u>?
 Ⓐ brick
 Ⓑ cloud
 Ⓒ train
 Ⓓ tame

3. What word begins with the same sound as <u>clamp</u>?
 Ⓐ cable
 Ⓑ clean
 Ⓒ cream
 Ⓓ keep

4. What word begins with the same sound as <u>glare</u>?
 Ⓐ glow
 Ⓑ game
 Ⓒ grow
 Ⓓ tear

| Name | Date |

5. What word has the same vowel sound as <u>apple</u>?
   Ⓐ cake
   Ⓑ pack
   Ⓒ ear
   Ⓓ home

6. What word has the same vowel sound as <u>tame</u>?
   Ⓐ page
   Ⓑ cup
   Ⓒ crib
   Ⓓ lack

7. What word has the same vowel sound as <u>jet</u>?
   Ⓐ beat
   Ⓑ cut
   Ⓒ come
   Ⓓ bet

8. What word has the same vowel sound as <u>here</u>?
   Ⓐ fear
   Ⓑ care
   Ⓒ her
   Ⓓ met

9. What word has the same vowel sound as <u>cup</u>?
   Ⓐ castle
   Ⓑ nut
   Ⓒ cute
   Ⓓ cape

10. What word has the same vowel sound as <u>mute</u>?
    Ⓐ cube
    Ⓑ yet
    Ⓒ cut
    Ⓓ mud

11. What word has the same vowel sound as <u>got</u>?
    Ⓐ open
    Ⓑ nose
    Ⓒ fog
    Ⓓ rat

12. What word has the same vowel sound as <u>bone</u>?
    Ⓐ pop
    Ⓑ ham
    Ⓒ cope
    Ⓓ bite

13. What word has the same vowel sound as sit?

    Ⓐ fight
    Ⓑ pat
    Ⓒ site
    Ⓓ him

14. What word has the same vowel sound as write?

    Ⓐ kite
    Ⓑ hit
    Ⓒ Jim
    Ⓓ ram

15. What word has the same ending sound as bunch?

    Ⓐ churn
    Ⓑ crunch
    Ⓒ blank
    Ⓓ wind

16. What word has the same ending sound as best?

    Ⓐ steak
    Ⓑ stand
    Ⓒ rest
    Ⓓ brave

17. What word has the same ending sound as grave?

    Ⓐ vest
    Ⓑ trade
    Ⓒ brave
    Ⓓ great

18. What word has the same ending sound as went?

    Ⓐ under
    Ⓑ lend
    Ⓒ tear
    Ⓓ bent

19. What word has the same sound as the underlined letters in hiding?

    Ⓐ going
    Ⓑ hid
    Ⓒ ran
    Ⓓ laughed

20. What word has the same sound as the underlined letters in scribble?

    Ⓐ catch
    Ⓑ cry
    Ⓒ describe
    Ⓓ don't

Name   Date

Word Recognition

Directions: Fill in the circle next to the word that has the same sound as the underlined letters.

Examples:

A. tr<u>ea</u>t
- ● meet
- Ⓑ every
- Ⓒ getting
- Ⓓ stuck

B. g<u>o</u>ing
- Ⓐ under
- Ⓑ camper
- ● open
- Ⓓ hotter

 Remember to fill in the circle for the word that has the same sound as the letter or letters that are underlined. Read carefully.

Practice

1. wh<u>ile</u>
   - Ⓐ tried
   - Ⓑ whale
   - Ⓒ file
   - Ⓓ hitter

2. pl<u>ea</u>se
   - Ⓐ saw
   - Ⓑ brief
   - Ⓒ plate
   - Ⓓ get

3. fu<u>dge</u>
   - Ⓐ yard
   - Ⓑ part
   - Ⓒ jump
   - Ⓓ dig

4. ging<u>er</u>
   - Ⓐ jet
   - Ⓑ dugout
   - Ⓒ tie
   - Ⓓ first

GO ON

Name   Date

5. <u>wr</u>eck
   - Ⓐ wrap
   - Ⓑ why
   - Ⓒ away
   - Ⓓ sack

6. tr<u>ee</u>
   - Ⓐ run
   - Ⓑ she
   - Ⓒ luck
   - Ⓓ tire

7. f<u>oo</u>d
   - Ⓐ outside
   - Ⓑ for
   - Ⓒ news
   - Ⓓ hog

8. <u>s</u>treet
   - Ⓐ stare
   - Ⓑ strike
   - Ⓒ heat
   - Ⓓ steep

9. dr<u>ai</u>n
   - Ⓐ glaze
   - Ⓑ bike
   - Ⓒ drink
   - Ⓓ rim

Directions: Fill in the circle next to the rhyming word.

10. hair
    - Ⓐ mare
    - Ⓑ him
    - Ⓒ ham
    - Ⓓ hard

11. plain
    - Ⓐ plaid
    - Ⓑ can
    - Ⓒ cane
    - Ⓓ plate

12. speech
    - Ⓐ speck
    - Ⓑ reach
    - Ⓒ cheap
    - Ⓓ pet

13. tale
    - Ⓐ mail
    - Ⓑ take
    - Ⓒ mud
    - Ⓓ tall

Name _____ Date _____

Word Skills

Directions: Fill in the circle next to each correct answer. Choose the correct vowel sound to complete each word.

Examples:

A. Choose the correct vowel sound to complete each word.   c__t

Ⓐ o   ● oa   Ⓒ a

B. Choose the correct word to complete each sentence. Susan is the _____ runner in the class.

Ⓐ fast   Ⓑ faster   ● fastest

Hint: Look at each choice carefully before choosing your answer.

Practice

1.  s__lboat

Ⓐ a   Ⓑ ai   Ⓒ au

3.  b__ch

Ⓐ ea   Ⓑ ei   Ⓒ e

2. 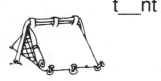 t__nt

Ⓐ u   Ⓑ i   Ⓒ e

4.  s__p

Ⓐ o   Ⓑ oo   Ⓒ oa

Name	Date

5. br__m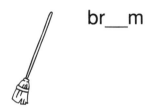

Ⓐ o Ⓑ oo Ⓒ oa

6.  g__t

Ⓐ o Ⓑ oa Ⓒ ou

7.  p__

Ⓐ ie Ⓑ i Ⓒ ey

8.  f__ld

Ⓐ e Ⓑ i Ⓒ ie

9. 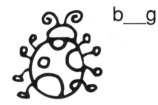 b__g

Ⓐ o Ⓑ oo Ⓒ u

10. 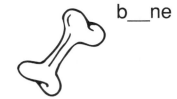 b__ne

Ⓐ oa Ⓑ o Ⓒ ou

11.  wh__le

Ⓐ a Ⓑ e Ⓒ ai

12. sh__

Ⓐ ue Ⓑ oo Ⓒ oe

Name   Date

Directions: Fill in the circle for the word that best completes each sentence.

13. I _____ my homework at home.
- Ⓐ lefted
- Ⓑ left
- Ⓒ let

14. We are _____ for many things at Thanksgiving.
- Ⓐ thankful
- Ⓑ thankless
- Ⓒ thank

15. Matt is the third _____.
- Ⓐ batted
- Ⓑ batting
- Ⓒ batter

16. Sarah is _____ in the race tomorrow.
- Ⓐ ran
- Ⓑ running
- Ⓒ runner

17. What time are you _____ to the party?
- Ⓐ go
- Ⓑ going
- Ⓒ went

18. I _____ Joe at the park yesterday.
- Ⓐ saw
- Ⓑ seen
- Ⓒ see

19. My mom will _____ us to school tomorrow.
- Ⓐ drived
- Ⓑ driving
- Ⓒ drive

20. Mary was very _____ when she carried the scissors.
- Ⓐ careful
- Ⓑ caring
- Ⓒ carefully

STOP

Name Date

Compound Words

Directions: Fill in the circle next to each compound word.

Examples:

A.
- Ⓐ shouldn't
- Ⓑ lunch
- Ⓒ better
- ● bedroom

B.
- ● rainbow
- Ⓑ Sally
- Ⓒ shoe
- Ⓓ lucky

 If you do not know an answer, skip the question and come back to it later.

Practice

1.
- Ⓐ joyful
- Ⓑ answer
- Ⓒ key
- Ⓓ broomstick

2.
- Ⓐ doorknob
- Ⓑ going
- Ⓒ week
- Ⓓ I'll

3.
- Ⓐ holiday
- Ⓑ weekend
- Ⓒ truck
- Ⓓ yellow

4.
- Ⓐ doctor
- Ⓑ under
- Ⓒ baseball
- Ⓓ taco

5.
- Ⓐ outside
- Ⓑ dinner
- Ⓒ like
- Ⓓ hunger

6.
- Ⓐ come
- Ⓑ never
- Ⓒ seaside
- Ⓓ ocean

7.
- Ⓐ gather
- Ⓑ playtime
- Ⓒ recess
- Ⓓ math

8.
- Ⓐ toolbox
- Ⓑ people
- Ⓒ friend
- Ⓓ can't

9.
- Ⓐ wouldn't
- Ⓑ helper
- Ⓒ popcorn
- Ⓓ time

10.
- Ⓐ crying
- Ⓑ happy
- Ⓒ butter
- Ⓓ birthday

11.
- Ⓐ tale
- Ⓑ turkey
- Ⓒ campsite
- Ⓓ funny

12.
- Ⓐ jellyfish
- Ⓑ shell
- Ⓒ packing
- Ⓓ upper

13.
- Ⓐ western
- Ⓑ roadside
- Ⓒ buzz
- Ⓓ wake

14.
- Ⓐ waterslide
- Ⓑ kitchen
- Ⓒ animal
- Ⓓ oldest

15.
- Ⓐ frame
- Ⓑ secret
- Ⓒ peanut
- Ⓓ calendar

16.
- Ⓐ date
- Ⓑ pineapple
- Ⓒ states
- Ⓓ curly

17.
- Ⓐ sorting
- Ⓑ hadn't
- Ⓒ shampoo
- Ⓓ sweatshirt

18.
- Ⓐ she'll
- Ⓑ places
- Ⓒ camera
- Ⓓ shoestring

19.
- Ⓐ sunshine
- Ⓑ period
- Ⓒ fluffy
- Ⓓ picture

20.
- Ⓐ phone
- Ⓑ candle
- Ⓒ lighter
- Ⓓ football

Name _____ Date _____

Contractions

Directions: Fill in the circle next to the word group that makes each contraction.

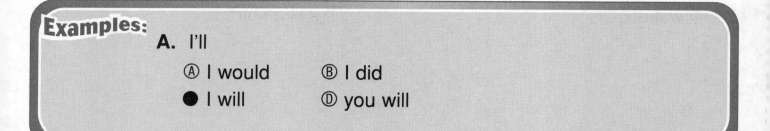

Examples:
A. I'll
- Ⓐ I would
- Ⓑ I did
- ● I will
- Ⓓ you will

Remember to choose only one answer for each question.

Practice

1. hadn't
   - Ⓐ have not
   - Ⓑ had not
   - Ⓒ did not
   - Ⓓ I did

2. we're
   - Ⓐ we are
   - Ⓑ we did
   - Ⓒ she did
   - Ⓓ it is

3. I've
   - Ⓐ we will
   - Ⓑ I have
   - Ⓒ I had
   - Ⓓ I will

4. you're
   - Ⓐ you will
   - Ⓑ you have
   - Ⓒ you are
   - Ⓓ he will

5. she'll
   - Ⓐ she is
   - Ⓑ he will
   - Ⓒ she will
   - Ⓓ she did

6. couldn't
   - Ⓐ could they
   - Ⓑ could not
   - Ⓒ would not
   - Ⓓ could it

7. it's
   - Ⓐ it tries
   - Ⓑ it lets
   - Ⓒ it is
   - Ⓓ it can

8. don't
   - Ⓐ do not
   - Ⓑ do get
   - Ⓒ can not
   - Ⓓ is not

9. we've
   - Ⓐ we save
   - Ⓑ we have
   - Ⓒ we did
   - Ⓓ we crawl

10. isn't
    - Ⓐ is she
    - Ⓑ is it
    - Ⓒ is not
    - Ⓓ do not

11. they'll
    - Ⓐ they call
    - Ⓑ they all
    - Ⓒ they did
    - Ⓓ they will

12. I'd
    - Ⓐ I would
    - Ⓑ I read
    - Ⓒ I will
    - Ⓓ I led

Name _____ Date _____

Contractions

Directions: Choose the correct contraction for each sentence.

Examples:

A. _____ enjoy this book.
- Ⓐ They've
- ● You'll
- Ⓒ Can't
- Ⓓ We've

 Read each sentence carefully before you choose your answer.

Practice

1. _____ go to the movie tomorrow.
   - Ⓐ You've
   - Ⓑ I've
   - Ⓒ Let's
   - Ⓓ You're

2. _____ reading that book now.
   - Ⓐ I'm
   - Ⓑ Let's
   - Ⓒ We've
   - Ⓓ You'll

3. She _____ stop the swing by herself.
   - Ⓐ it's
   - Ⓑ haven't
   - Ⓒ can't
   - Ⓓ hadn't

4. _____ leaving at 9 a.m.
   - Ⓐ We're
   - Ⓑ She'll
   - Ⓒ We'll
   - Ⓓ You've

5. Jack _____ know the answer to the problem.
   - Ⓐ haven't
   - Ⓑ wasn't
   - Ⓒ didn't
   - Ⓓ hasn't

6. _____ given Sue directions to the game.
   - Ⓐ She'll
   - Ⓑ I've
   - Ⓒ I'll
   - Ⓓ Let's

| Name | Date |

Root Words, Prefixes, and Suffixes

Directions: Fill in the circle next to the correct root or base word.

Examples:

A. unlikely
- ● like
- Ⓑ un
- Ⓒ likely
- Ⓓ ly

B. running
- Ⓐ ing
- Ⓑ runner
- ● run
- Ⓓ un

 Look carefully at each choice. If you get confused after you have answered a question, stay with your first choice.

Practice

1. careful
   - Ⓐ ful
   - Ⓑ car
   - Ⓒ care
   - Ⓓ are

2. highest
   - Ⓐ high
   - Ⓑ igh
   - Ⓒ est
   - Ⓓ hig

3. crowded
   - Ⓐ ed
   - Ⓑ crow
   - Ⓒ crowd
   - Ⓓ ded

4. thinking
   - Ⓐ ink
   - Ⓑ think
   - Ⓒ ing
   - Ⓓ hin

GO ON

Name _____ Date _____

5. gotten
   Ⓐ ten
   Ⓑ en
   Ⓒ got
   Ⓓ go

6. fearless
   Ⓐ ear
   Ⓑ fear
   Ⓒ less
   Ⓓ earl

7. caller
   Ⓐ call
   Ⓑ er
   Ⓒ ler
   Ⓓ all

8. helpful
   Ⓐ elp
   Ⓑ ful
   Ⓒ help
   Ⓓ elpful

9. unwrap
   Ⓐ rap
   Ⓑ un
   Ⓒ wra
   Ⓓ wrap

10. slowest
    Ⓐ slow
    Ⓑ low
    Ⓒ est
    Ⓓ ow

11. unhappy
    Ⓐ hap
    Ⓑ un
    Ⓒ py
    Ⓓ happy

12. played
    Ⓐ yed
    Ⓑ play
    Ⓒ lay
    Ⓓ ed

Name _____ Date _____

Root Words, Prefixes, and Suffixes

Directions: Fill in the circle that shows the correct prefix or suffix for each word.

Examples:

A. undo
- Ⓐ do
- ● un
- Ⓒ und
- Ⓓ nd

B. helper
- Ⓐ help
- Ⓑ elp
- ● er
- Ⓓ per

Remember to look for the prefix or suffix on each word.

Practice

1. dialing
   - Ⓐ dial
   - Ⓑ ling
   - Ⓒ di
   - Ⓓ ing

2. sheepish
   - Ⓐ sh
   - Ⓑ pish
   - Ⓒ sheep
   - Ⓓ ish

3. forgetful
   - Ⓐ get
   - Ⓑ for
   - Ⓒ ful
   - Ⓓ forget

4. sunless
   - Ⓐ sun
   - Ⓑ less
   - Ⓒ un
   - Ⓓ unles

Name _____ Date _____

5. fighter
   Ⓐ er
   Ⓑ ight
   Ⓒ fi
   Ⓓ fight

6. fixable
   Ⓐ fix
   Ⓑ able
   Ⓒ le
   Ⓓ fi

7. likely
   Ⓐ ly
   Ⓑ like
   Ⓒ li
   Ⓓ ike

8. braiding
   Ⓐ br
   Ⓑ ing
   Ⓒ aid
   Ⓓ braid

9. fastest
   Ⓐ fast
   Ⓑ test
   Ⓒ est
   Ⓓ fas

10. trainer
    Ⓐ tr
    Ⓑ rain
    Ⓒ train
    Ⓓ er

11. girlish
    Ⓐ ish
    Ⓑ lish
    Ⓒ girl
    Ⓓ gir

12. likeable
    Ⓐ li
    Ⓑ like
    Ⓒ able
    Ⓓ le

STOP

Test Prep Connection—Grade 2—RBP0857   www.summerbridgeactivities.com   ©RBP Books

Sample Test

Directions: Fill in the circle next to the word that has the same beginning or ending sound as the underlined letters.

1. <u>d</u>rum
   - Ⓐ track
   - Ⓑ drama
   - Ⓒ great

2. <u>p</u>ress
   - Ⓐ price
   - Ⓑ pore
   - Ⓒ grass

3. bun<u>ch</u>
   - Ⓐ trench
   - Ⓑ greet
   - Ⓒ bunk

4. pa<u>ck</u>
   - Ⓐ crumb
   - Ⓑ punt
   - Ⓒ crack

Directions: Fill in the circle next to the word that has the same vowel sound as the underlined word.

5. <u>box</u>
   - Ⓐ hockey
   - Ⓑ yikes
   - Ⓒ boat

6. <u>hide</u>
   - Ⓐ for
   - Ⓑ bye
   - Ⓒ hit

7. <u>able</u>
   - Ⓐ hat
   - Ⓑ jack
   - Ⓒ rate

GO ON

Name _____ Date _____

Directions: Fill in the circle next to the word that rhymes with each picture.

Directions: Fill in the circle next to the correct letter or letters that complete the word for the picture.

8.

Ⓐ box Ⓑ star Ⓒ rag

11. fr__me

Ⓐ e Ⓑ u
Ⓒ a Ⓓ ai

9.

Ⓐ course Ⓑ cow Ⓒ bike

12. b__

Ⓐ oi Ⓑ o
Ⓒ oy Ⓓ y

10.

Ⓐ rainbow Ⓑ beach Ⓒ car

13. ch__se

Ⓐ ea Ⓑ e
Ⓒ ei Ⓓ ee

GO ON

Test Prep Connection—Grade 2—RBP0857 www.summerbridgeactivities.com ©RBP Books

Name _____   Date _____

Directions: Fill in the circle for the word that completes each sentence.

14. Jane is very _____ when she checks her work.
  Ⓐ carefully Ⓑ careful
  Ⓒ care Ⓓ fully

15. The vegetables in the salad were _____.
  Ⓐ freshed Ⓑ fresher
  Ⓒ fresh Ⓓ freshful

16. Kitty _____ me to a sleepover.
  Ⓐ invited Ⓑ invite
  Ⓒ inviting Ⓓ inviter

17. I went to the park to _____ my dog.
  Ⓐ walking Ⓑ walker
  Ⓒ walk Ⓓ walked

Directions: Fill in the circle next to each compound word.

18.
  Ⓐ skater Ⓑ skateboard
  Ⓒ boarder Ⓓ skate

19.
  Ⓐ cheer Ⓑ leader
  Ⓒ cheerleader Ⓓ cheerer

20.
  Ⓐ doghouse Ⓑ dog
  Ⓒ house Ⓓ dogger

21.
  Ⓐ beat Ⓑ heart
  Ⓒ hearts Ⓓ heartbeat

22.
  Ⓐ under Ⓑ underground
  Ⓒ ground Ⓓ grounds

23.
  Ⓐ beachfront Ⓑ fronts
  Ⓒ beacher Ⓓ beaches

| Name | Date |

Directions: Fill in the compound word that matches each picture.

24.

- Ⓐ surfer
- Ⓑ surfboard
- Ⓒ rainbow

25.

- Ⓐ pool
- Ⓑ diver
- Ⓒ swimsuit

26.

- Ⓐ pillowcase
- Ⓑ bed
- Ⓒ pillow

Directions: Fill in the circle next to the words that make each contraction.

27. let's
- Ⓐ let hers
- Ⓑ let his
- Ⓒ let us
- Ⓓ let they

28. it'd
- Ⓐ it would
- Ⓑ it can
- Ⓒ it fed
- Ⓓ she did

29. wasn't
- Ⓐ was plant
- Ⓑ was not
- Ⓒ was can
- Ⓓ was did

30. they've
- Ⓐ they were
- Ⓑ they did
- Ⓒ they like
- Ⓓ they have

Name _____ Date _____

Directions: Fill in the circle next to correct root or base word.

31. jumping
- Ⓐ ing
- Ⓑ jum
- Ⓒ jump
- Ⓓ jumper

32. kisser
- Ⓐ kissing
- Ⓑ kiss
- Ⓒ kisses
- Ⓓ er

33. calls
- Ⓐ calling
- Ⓑ caller
- Ⓒ call
- Ⓓ all

34. heater
- Ⓐ eat
- Ⓑ er
- Ⓒ heats
- Ⓓ heat

35. going
- Ⓐ go
- Ⓑ goed
- Ⓒ ing
- Ⓓ oi

36. played
- Ⓐ ed
- Ⓑ play
- Ⓒ yed
- Ⓓ pl

37. watched
- Ⓐ ed
- Ⓑ tch
- Ⓒ ched
- Ⓓ watch

38. cleaning
- Ⓐ lean
- Ⓑ ning
- Ⓒ clean
- Ⓓ ing

Name   Date

Picture Vocabulary

Directions: Fill in the circle next to the word that matches each picture.

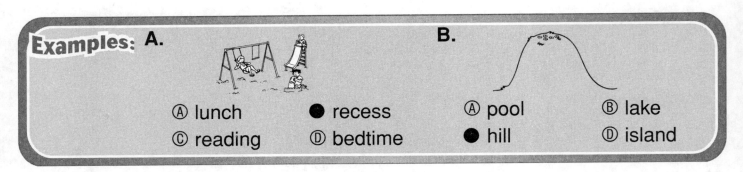

Examples:

A.
- Ⓐ lunch
- ● recess
- Ⓒ reading
- Ⓓ bedtime

B.
- Ⓐ pool
- Ⓑ lake
- ● hill
- Ⓓ island

Hint: Look at each picture carefully. Read each choice before you make your final decision.

Practice

1.
   - Ⓐ yard
   - Ⓑ desk
   - Ⓒ computer
   - Ⓓ paper

3.
   - Ⓐ water
   - Ⓑ outside
   - Ⓒ pool
   - Ⓓ fun

2.
   - Ⓐ plate
   - Ⓑ garage
   - Ⓒ match
   - Ⓓ candle

4.
   - Ⓐ cuddle
   - Ⓑ baby
   - Ⓒ children
   - Ⓓ small

GO ON

Name _____   Date _____

5.

   Ⓐ book   Ⓑ music
   Ⓒ reading   Ⓓ band

6.

   Ⓐ truck   Ⓑ car
   Ⓒ wheels   Ⓓ drive

7.

   Ⓐ bed   Ⓑ quilt
   Ⓒ sleepy   Ⓓ cold

8.

   Ⓐ sofa   Ⓑ sitting
   Ⓒ chair   Ⓓ hard

9.

   Ⓐ homework   Ⓑ children
   Ⓒ cafeteria   Ⓓ school

10.

    Ⓐ blinds   Ⓑ look
    Ⓒ wood   Ⓓ home

11.

    Ⓐ soap   Ⓑ dirty
    Ⓒ clean   Ⓓ washing

12.

    Ⓐ farm   Ⓑ city
    Ⓒ news   Ⓓ forest

STOP

Name _____ Date _____

Vocabulary Skills

Directions: Fill in the circle next to the best answer.

Examples: A. Something you hang on the wall is a…
Ⓐ bag   ● picture
Ⓒ tablecloth   Ⓓ basket

B. Something you take to school is a…
● pencil   Ⓑ box
Ⓒ shell   Ⓓ tree

   Look for important words in each question.

Practice

1. Something you use at the beach is…
   Ⓐ sunscreen   Ⓑ ice skates
   Ⓒ heater   Ⓓ jacket

2. Something you plant in a garden is…
   Ⓐ dirt   Ⓑ flowers
   Ⓒ wood   Ⓓ water

3. Something that happened yesterday is in the…
   Ⓐ past   Ⓑ future
   Ⓒ present   Ⓓ tomorrow

4. Something not done correctly is…
   Ⓐ good   Ⓑ wrong
   Ⓒ right   Ⓓ ugly

5. Part of your body is your…
   Ⓐ book   Ⓑ ring
   Ⓒ bow   Ⓓ spine

6. One way to exercise is to…
   Ⓐ sleep   Ⓑ eat
   Ⓒ run   Ⓓ drink

7. A covering for a table is a…
   - Ⓐ sheet
   - Ⓑ pillow
   - Ⓒ bed skirt
   - Ⓓ tablecloth

8. You order food in a…
   - Ⓐ restaurant
   - Ⓑ taxi
   - Ⓒ home
   - Ⓓ park

9. A place where you visit animals is a…
   - Ⓐ yard
   - Ⓑ zoo
   - Ⓒ playground
   - Ⓓ school

10. If you like to do something, it is…
    - Ⓐ careful
    - Ⓑ thoughtless
    - Ⓒ enjoyable
    - Ⓓ hateful

11. Planes, trains, and cars are types of…
    - Ⓐ tricks
    - Ⓑ transportation
    - Ⓒ evaporation
    - Ⓓ communication

12. Someone in your family is a…
    - Ⓐ relative
    - Ⓑ pilot
    - Ⓒ friend
    - Ⓓ neighbor

13. Something you may see in the night sky is the…
    - Ⓐ sun
    - Ⓑ moon
    - Ⓒ waves
    - Ⓓ checkers

14. You pay for things with…
    - Ⓐ shells
    - Ⓑ water
    - Ⓒ money
    - Ⓓ time

15. To look for something is to…
    - Ⓐ wander
    - Ⓑ hide
    - Ⓒ lose
    - Ⓓ search

Name _____ Date _____

Synonyms

Directions: Read each sentence. Fill in the circle next to the synonym for each underlined word.

Examples:

A. Julie was <u>terrible</u> in the grocery store with her mother.
 ● bad   Ⓑ nice
 Ⓒ ugly   Ⓓ good

B. Would you please <u>lower</u> the lights in the kitchen?
 Ⓐ bright   Ⓑ change
 ● dim   Ⓓ raise

 You are looking for words that have a similar meaning to the underlined word.

Practice

1. I was <u>scared</u> of the haunted house.
   Ⓐ happy   Ⓑ frightened
   Ⓒ glad   Ⓓ yikes

2. The lake house was very <u>beautiful</u>.
   Ⓐ ugly   Ⓑ liked
   Ⓒ lovely   Ⓓ neat

3. The clothes got <u>wet</u> in the rainstorm.
   Ⓐ dry   Ⓑ dirty
   Ⓒ clean   Ⓓ soaked

4. I am in the <u>final</u> chapter of the book.
   Ⓐ last   Ⓑ first
   Ⓒ middle   Ⓓ third

5. The new job will <u>relocate</u> us to a new city.
   Ⓐ keep   Ⓑ move
   Ⓒ try   Ⓓ turn

6. The teacher could not read the <u>sloppy</u> handwriting.
   Ⓐ neat   Ⓑ nice
   Ⓒ messy   Ⓓ tired

7. Jim was overjoyed as he rode his new horse.
   Ⓐ sad
   Ⓑ silly
   Ⓒ hurting
   Ⓓ excited

8. Susan found a simple way to understand the math problem.
   Ⓐ easy
   Ⓑ hard
   Ⓒ difficult
   Ⓓ nice

9. The toddler was mean to the babysitter.
   Ⓐ neat
   Ⓑ kind
   Ⓒ sweet
   Ⓓ rude

10. We always leave the classroom clean at the end of the day.
    Ⓐ messy
    Ⓑ tidy
    Ⓒ dirty
    Ⓓ full

11. The soil was damp after the rain.
    Ⓐ clean
    Ⓑ dry
    Ⓒ moist
    Ⓓ dirty

12. The baby was sleepy after playing in the park.
    Ⓐ tired
    Ⓑ awake
    Ⓒ choppy
    Ⓓ cranky

13. It was amazing to see the stars in the sky.
    Ⓐ unlikely
    Ⓑ nice
    Ⓒ fascinating
    Ⓓ enjoyable

14. Mike's room was very neat and orderly.
    Ⓐ messy
    Ⓑ sloppy
    Ⓒ blue
    Ⓓ organized

Name _____ Date _____

Antonyms

Directions: Fill in the circle next to the word that is an antonym for the underlined word.

Examples:

A. The flower arrangement looked <u>pretty</u>.
- Ⓐ nice
- Ⓑ neat
- ● ugly
- Ⓓ lovely

B. Please turn <u>on</u> the lights.
- ● off
- Ⓑ under
- Ⓒ like
- Ⓓ onto

You are looking for the word that means the <u>opposite</u> of the underlined word. Choose the best answer.

Practice

1. We climbed <u>up</u> the hill in one hour.
   - Ⓐ down
   - Ⓑ over
   - Ⓒ under
   - Ⓓ high

2. I <u>always</u> wear my lucky shirt on game day.
   - Ⓐ like to
   - Ⓑ never
   - Ⓒ sometimes
   - Ⓓ once

3. The bath water was too <u>cold</u> for the baby.
   - Ⓐ warm
   - Ⓑ chilly
   - Ⓒ cool
   - Ⓓ hot

4. Look <u>under</u> the bed for the lost shoe.
   - Ⓐ beneath
   - Ⓑ above
   - Ⓒ along
   - Ⓓ in

5. The weather was <u>rainy</u> all day.
   - Ⓐ nasty
   - Ⓑ ugly
   - Ⓒ sunny
   - Ⓓ pretty

6. Susan will <u>finish</u> the book next week.
   - Ⓐ end
   - Ⓑ finalize
   - Ⓒ practice
   - Ⓓ start

Name _____ Date _____

7. Let's <u>walk</u> to the store.
   Ⓐ run
   Ⓑ jump
   Ⓒ stroll
   Ⓓ skip

8. Rick cheers <u>against</u> the blue team.
   Ⓐ on
   Ⓑ to
   Ⓒ for
   Ⓓ toward

9. The server gave me a <u>full</u> glass of water.
   Ⓐ empty
   Ⓑ halfway
   Ⓒ yellow
   Ⓓ tall

10. I like to sleep with a <u>soft</u> pillow.
    Ⓐ cushion
    Ⓑ hard
    Ⓒ difficult
    Ⓓ tight

11. You should not <u>shout</u> inside the library.
    Ⓐ yell
    Ⓑ scream
    Ⓒ whisper
    Ⓓ talk

12. Turn <u>right</u> at the traffic light.
    Ⓐ around
    Ⓑ up
    Ⓒ straight
    Ⓓ left

13. The race will <u>begin</u> at noon.
    Ⓐ end
    Ⓑ start
    Ⓒ take off
    Ⓓ go

14. Taylor <u>hates</u> to exercise.
    Ⓐ wishes
    Ⓑ wants
    Ⓒ loves
    Ⓓ dislikes

STOP

Name _____ Date _____

Homonyms

Directions: Some words sound alike but are spelled differently. Fill in the circle next to the word that correctly completes each sentence.

Example:

A. I don't know _____ way to go.
- ● which
- Ⓑ witch

Think about each answer carefully before you make your decision.

Practice

1. My mother doesn't like to _____ food.
   - Ⓐ waist
   - Ⓑ waste

2. I would like another _____ of pie.
   - Ⓐ piece
   - Ⓑ peace

3. Jill bought a new _____ of shoes yesterday.
   - Ⓐ pear
   - Ⓑ pair

4. I _____ that from kindergarten.
   - Ⓐ know
   - Ⓑ no

5. Steve tied a _____ in his shoelace.
   - Ⓐ knot
   - Ⓑ not

6. Turn _____ at the stoplight.
   - Ⓐ write
   - Ⓑ right

Name _____ Date _____

Multi-Meaning Words

Directions: Some words are spelled the same and sound the same but have different meanings. Fill in the circle next to the word that completes both sentences correctly.

Example: A. Millie loves to _____ down the hill.
I ate a _____ with dinner last night.
  Ⓐ jump   ● roll
  Ⓒ hike   Ⓓ tart

 Read both sentences before you choose your answer.

Practice

1. We lit the fire with a _____.
   Julie's shoes will _____ her dress.
   Ⓐ flame   Ⓑ go
   Ⓒ match   Ⓓ light

2. Please _____ me the book on the table.
   Jack cut his _____ on the metal.
   Ⓐ foot   Ⓑ hand
   Ⓒ pass   Ⓓ arm

3. I ate a _____ of cereal for breakfast.
   Hank and Sue like to _____ on Saturdays.
   Ⓐ play   Ⓑ plate
   Ⓒ bowl   Ⓓ dance

4. There was one _____ in the pond.
   Ray had to _____ his head going under the tree.
   Ⓐ duck   Ⓑ move
   Ⓒ pet   Ⓓ rake

5. Dad will use one _____ to hang the picture.
   Mom broke her _____ moving the furniture.
   Ⓐ hammer   Ⓑ try
   Ⓒ earring   Ⓓ nail

6. Ms. Campbell needs to _____ after the trip.
   We ate the _____ of the candy.
   Ⓐ play   Ⓑ most
   Ⓒ rest   Ⓓ whole

Name _____ Date _____

Words in Context

Directions: Fill in the circle next to the word that best completes each sentence.

Examples: A. The trees swayed back and forth in the _____.
- Ⓐ sunlight
- Ⓑ forest
- Ⓒ nighttime
- ● thunderstorm

B. The children found lots of seashells on the _____.
- ● beach
- Ⓑ river
- Ⓒ lake
- Ⓓ desert

 Use the clues from each sentence to help you find the correct answer.

Practice

1. Hang the picture in the middle of the _____.
   - Ⓐ door
   - Ⓑ window
   - Ⓒ wall
   - Ⓓ chair

2. Let's plant the _____ in the garden at noon.
   - Ⓐ trash
   - Ⓑ flowers
   - Ⓒ yard
   - Ⓓ water

3. I have _____ to help us get to the party.
   - Ⓐ symbols
   - Ⓑ streets
   - Ⓒ directions
   - Ⓓ time

4. She wants her hair _____, but it is curly.
   - Ⓐ long
   - Ⓑ straight
   - Ⓒ short
   - Ⓓ natural

GO ON

Name _____ Date _____

5. The new _____ will help you feel better when you are sick.
   Ⓐ bed
   Ⓑ medicine
   Ⓒ crayons
   Ⓓ hospital

6. We like to go _____ in the winter.
   Ⓐ snowboarding
   Ⓑ swimming
   Ⓒ surfing
   Ⓓ biking

7. The _____ kept the sun out of my eyes.
   Ⓐ shirt
   Ⓑ cover
   Ⓒ sunglasses
   Ⓓ car

8. The scented candle made the room _____ nice.
   Ⓐ look
   Ⓑ smell
   Ⓒ taste
   Ⓓ like

9. Please ring the _____ when you arrive.
   Ⓐ doorbell
   Ⓑ telephone
   Ⓒ television
   Ⓓ knock

10. You should always wear a _____ when you ride your bike.
    Ⓐ hat
    Ⓑ shirt
    Ⓒ helmet
    Ⓓ skate

11. Emma hangs her clothes in a large _____.
    Ⓐ car
    Ⓑ closet
    Ⓒ hamper
    Ⓓ chest

12. There are many tall _____ in the city.
    Ⓐ buildings
    Ⓑ homes
    Ⓒ trees
    Ⓓ sidewalks

STOP

Name _____   Date _____

Sample Test

Directions: Fill in the circle next to the word that matches the picture.

1.

- Ⓐ instrument
- Ⓑ band
- Ⓒ game
- Ⓓ drum

2.

- Ⓐ melting
- Ⓑ cold
- Ⓒ hot
- Ⓓ light

3.

- Ⓐ day
- Ⓑ tomorrow
- Ⓒ night
- Ⓓ flight

4.

- Ⓐ city
- Ⓑ farm
- Ⓒ tree
- Ⓓ island

Test Prep Connection—Grade 2—RBP0857   www.summerbridgeactivities.com   ©RBP Books

Name _____ Date _____

Directions: Fill in the circle next to the best answer.

5. To get ready to do something is to...
   Ⓐ hover
   Ⓑ travel
   Ⓒ prepare
   Ⓓ progress

6. To go somewhere and then come home is to...
   Ⓐ visit
   Ⓑ leave
   Ⓒ remove
   Ⓓ hide

7. Someone who commits a crime is a...
   Ⓐ florist
   Ⓑ criminal
   Ⓒ keeper
   Ⓓ runner

8. To make something new is to...
   Ⓐ copy
   Ⓑ reply
   Ⓒ invent
   Ⓓ invite

Directions: Fill in the circle next to the word that is a synonym for the underlined word.

9. Were you afraid of the old house?
   Ⓐ happy
   Ⓑ frightened
   Ⓒ nervous
   Ⓓ amazed

10. The teacher gave us a tough test on Wednesday.
    Ⓐ easy
    Ⓑ expensive
    Ⓒ difficult
    Ⓓ fun

11. Pet the new kitten softly.
    Ⓐ hard
    Ⓑ roughly
    Ⓒ kindly
    Ⓓ gently

12. Place the cup on the highest shelf.
    Ⓐ lowest
    Ⓑ bottom
    Ⓒ top
    Ⓓ middle

Name _____ Date _____

Directions: Fill in the circle next to the word that is an antonym for each underlined word.

13. Let's go <u>inside</u> and play.
   Ⓐ outside
   Ⓑ upstairs
   Ⓒ over
   Ⓓ hiding

14. He was extremely <u>tall</u> for a basketball player.
   Ⓐ long
   Ⓑ nice
   Ⓒ short
   Ⓓ mean

15. You should always keep your bedroom <u>messy</u>.
   Ⓐ cluttered
   Ⓑ unorganized
   Ⓒ clean
   Ⓓ pretty

16. The kitchen is <u>upstairs</u>.
   Ⓐ up
   Ⓑ outside
   Ⓒ under
   Ⓓ downstairs

Directions: Fill in the circle next to the word that correctly completes each sentence.

17. I would like _____ orders of French fries.
   Ⓐ too   Ⓑ two

18. Laurie had already _____ the movie.
   Ⓐ seen   Ⓑ scene

19. Jeff _____ his bike on the first day of school.
   Ⓐ road   Ⓑ rode

20. Someone spotted a black _____ in the mountains.
   Ⓐ bear   Ⓑ bare

Name _____ Date _____

Directions: Fill in the circle next to the word that completes both sentences correctly.

21. The _____ change colors and fall off the trees in the fall.
    Mom _____ for the station at noon.
    Ⓐ tree   Ⓑ left
    Ⓒ leaves   Ⓓ ground

22. Susan can _____ any situation.
    Turn the _____ to get inside.
    Ⓐ handle   Ⓑ identify
    Ⓒ knob   Ⓓ fix

23. She wore the _____ on her left hand.
    I made a _____ in the sand with a stick.
    Ⓐ bracelet Ⓑ circle
    Ⓒ stone   Ⓓ ring

24. The ballet dancer wore her hair in a _____.
    I like mustard on my hamburger _____.
    Ⓐ knot   Ⓑ side
    Ⓒ bun   Ⓓ please

Directions: Fill in the circle next to the word that best completes each sentence.

25. The dog _____ the cat around the house four times.
    Ⓐ ran   Ⓑ moved
    Ⓒ chased   Ⓓ pushed

26. In January many people join _____ for exercise.
    Ⓐ lakes   Ⓑ pools
    Ⓒ gyms   Ⓓ tracks

27. Kyle is in second grade. He is _____ years old.
    Ⓐ seven   Ⓑ two
    Ⓒ seventy   Ⓓ seventeen

28. Mark had poor eyesight. He got _____ to help him see better.
    Ⓐ jackets   Ⓑ glasses
    Ⓒ shoes   Ⓓ a hat

29. We live two miles from the beach. It takes us about _____ minutes to drive to the ocean.
    Ⓐ fifty   Ⓑ fifteen
    Ⓒ five   Ⓓ thirty

Name _____ Date _____

Picture Comprehension

Directions: Use the picture to help you answer the questions below. Fill in the circle next to the best answer.

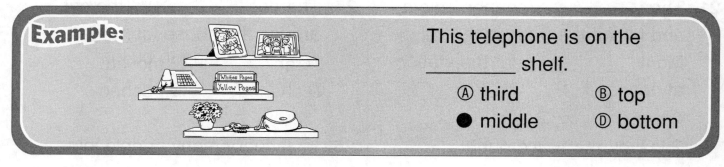

Example: This telephone is on the _____ shelf.
Ⓐ third   Ⓑ top
● middle   Ⓓ bottom

 Think about what is happening in the picture to help you answer the questions.

Practice

1. The children are going inside the _____.
   Ⓐ bank   Ⓑ library
   Ⓒ school   Ⓓ supermarket

2. They are buying _____ and cheese for their mom.
   Ⓐ cards   Ⓑ video games
   Ⓒ milk   Ⓓ cell phones

3. They will pay with _____.
   Ⓐ gas   Ⓑ money
   Ⓒ books   Ⓓ food

4. Jack's mom is helping him get bundled up because it is _____ outside.
   Ⓐ cold   Ⓑ cool
   Ⓒ hot   Ⓓ warm

5. He is meeting his friends outside to go _____.
   Ⓐ ice skating
   Ⓑ sledding
   Ⓒ snowboarding
   Ⓓ skateboarding

6. Jack is _____ to go outside and meet his friends.
   - Ⓐ excited
   - Ⓑ sad
   - Ⓒ lonely
   - Ⓓ fearful

7. John is waiting for the _____.
   - Ⓐ train
   - Ⓑ bus
   - Ⓒ airplane
   - Ⓓ race

8. It will take him to _____.
   - Ⓐ school
   - Ⓑ his grandmother's
   - Ⓒ church
   - Ⓓ eat

9. John will see his _____ at school.
   - Ⓐ dog
   - Ⓑ baby brother
   - Ⓒ teacher
   - Ⓓ mom

10. Tanner is going to build a _____.
    - Ⓐ tightrope
    - Ⓑ sandcastle
    - Ⓒ water park
    - Ⓓ rainbow

11. He will have a _____ time today.
    - Ⓐ miserable
    - Ⓑ scary
    - Ⓒ terrible
    - Ⓓ fantastic

12. Tanner will ask his _____ to help him.
    - Ⓐ puppy
    - Ⓑ baby sister
    - Ⓒ dad
    - Ⓓ doll

Name	Date

Critical Reading

Directions: Read each sentence. Fill in the circle next to the sentence that could <u>not</u> happen.

Example:
- Ⓐ Molly and I took the dog for a walk in the park.
- Ⓑ We saw Mark with his dog.
- ● The dogs took off on a spaceship to outer space.
- Ⓓ We had a quick conversation with Mark.

 Remember, you are looking for the sentence that could <u>not</u> happen.

Practice

1.
- Ⓐ There was a great movie on television last night.
- Ⓑ I watched it with my mother.
- Ⓒ The characters came through the television and talked to us.
- Ⓓ The movie took place in Kansas.

2.
- Ⓐ Our class took a field trip to the zoo.
- Ⓑ We saw lots of animals.
- Ⓒ The animals asked us to have lunch with them.
- Ⓓ We ate lunch back at school.

3.
- Ⓐ I took the train to see my grandmother.
- Ⓑ I visited with my grandmother for three weeks.
- Ⓒ We had a lots of fun.
- Ⓓ I took a spaceship home.

4.
- Ⓐ Some people enjoy dancing for exercise.
- Ⓑ There are many different types of dancing.
- Ⓒ I saw two elephants dancing in the park.
- Ⓓ People often dance at parties.

Name   Date

Critical Reading

Directions: Read each sentence. Fill in the circle next to the sentence that could happen.

Example:
- ● I went to the ocean with my family.
- Ⓑ When we got there, the ocean had disappeared.
- Ⓒ The jellyfish told us not to worry because the ocean would be back tomorrow.
- Ⓓ We waited until the next day, and the ocean came back.

 Remember, this time you are looking for the sentence that <u>could</u> happen.

Practice

1.
- Ⓐ Two unicorns were waiting at the subway stop.
- Ⓑ The unicorns were talking about the weather.
- Ⓒ I took the subway downtown.
- Ⓓ The unicorns got off the subway at the second stop.

2.
- Ⓐ The alien spaceship landed on Jupiter in June.
- Ⓑ The aliens took lots of pictures of the planet.
- Ⓒ The aliens brought the pictures to show us.
- Ⓓ We watched a movie about space in school.

3.
- Ⓐ We took a walk in the forest.
- Ⓑ The trees were telling us a story about the rain.
- Ⓒ The rain told us a story about the flowers.
- Ⓓ The flowers were not happy and flew away.

4.
- Ⓐ The letters in the mailbox were discussing where they were being sent.
- Ⓑ I mailed four letters yesterday.
- Ⓒ One letter told another letter that she was sad because she would miss being friends.
- Ⓓ The letters said good-bye to the mailbox.

Name _____ Date _____

Story Comprehension

Directions: Read each story. Fill in the circle next to the best answer for each question.

Example: Allie was meeting Kate at the park. She told her mom good-bye; then she put on her helmet. Allie and Kate had fun at the park.
What were Allie and Kate probably doing at the park?

Ⓐ hiking
● bike-riding
Ⓒ building sandcastles
Ⓓ picking flowers

Go back to the story to help you answer the questions.

Practice

"I do not know what costume I will wear to the party," said Cal.

"Why don't you dress up in your turtle costume?" asked Cal's dad. "You are sure to be a hit in that."

"Yeah," said Cal, "but I really want to win the grand prize for the scariest costume, and I don't think the turtle costume is that scary."

"How about the scary vampire costume your brother wore a few years ago? That one really scared some people."

"That's perfect, Dad. Where is it?"

"Up in the attic. Let's go get it."

1. Where is Cal most likely going?

   Ⓐ Halloween party
   Ⓑ Christmas party
   Ⓒ birthday party
   Ⓓ spring break party

2. Who wore the vampire costume before Cal?

   Ⓐ his mom   Ⓑ his dad
   Ⓒ his brother   Ⓓ his dog

Name _____ Date _____

Matter

Matter is all around us. Matter is anything that takes up space and has mass. There are three different states of matter: solid, liquid, and gas. Solids cannot move on their own, and they have their own shape. A stuffed animal is an example of a solid. Liquids take the shape of their container. An example of a liquid is orange juice. Gases do not have a definite shape, and they fill their container. Examples of gases are air in a balloon and steam coming from a cup of coffee.

Matter can go through two types of changes: physical and chemical. Physical changes only change what the matter looks like. If you cut a tomato in half, you still have a tomato. It may be cut in two, but it will still taste and smell the same. Chemical changes in matter will change the identity of the matter. An example of a chemical change is iron rusting.

Matter is described by its properties. A property may be color, shape, size, weight, or texture. Properties define matter, and matter defines the world in which we live.

1. The author wrote this to _____.
   - Ⓐ make you laugh
   - Ⓑ inform you
   - Ⓒ persuade you
   - Ⓓ make you cry

2. _____ describe matter.
   - Ⓐ Properties
   - Ⓑ Solids
   - Ⓒ Gases
   - Ⓓ Changes

3. Orange juice is a _____.
   - Ⓐ change
   - Ⓑ solid
   - Ⓒ liquid
   - Ⓓ color

4. Solids, liquids, and gases are all states of _____.
   - Ⓐ matter
   - Ⓑ chemical changes
   - Ⓒ form
   - Ⓓ properties

5. Cutting a head of lettuce in half is an example of a _____ change.
   - Ⓐ chemical
   - Ⓑ funny
   - Ⓒ colorful
   - Ⓓ physical

6. _____ is anything that takes up space and has mass.
   - Ⓐ Matter
   - Ⓑ Change
   - Ⓒ Property
   - Ⓓ Liquid

STOP

Dear Classmates,

My name is Emma. I am running for class president. I have been a student at Woodberry Elementary School since kindergarten.

If you vote for me as class president, I will work hard to keep the restrooms clean for us at school. I will also fight to put pizza on the menu every day!

Vote for Emma as class president!

Thank you!

Emma

1. Emma is _____.
   Ⓐ running for class president
   Ⓑ taking a test
   Ⓒ the class clown
   Ⓓ ten years old

2. Emma has been a student at Woodberry Elementary School since _____.
   Ⓐ first grade
   Ⓑ kindergarten
   Ⓒ last year
   Ⓓ third grade

3. This letter is written to _____.
   Ⓐ make you laugh
   Ⓑ persuade you to do something
   Ⓒ your mom
   Ⓓ the principal

4. If Emma is voted as class president, she wants to _____.
   Ⓐ build a new playground
   Ⓑ change schools
   Ⓒ keep the restrooms clean for the students
   Ⓓ add grilled cheese to the menu every day

Name _____   Date _____

Sample Test

Directions: Fill in the circle next to the best answer.

1. These children are most likely going _____.

   Ⓐ fishing   Ⓑ bowling
   Ⓒ swimming   Ⓓ rollerblading

2. These children are most likely celebrating _____.

   Ⓐ school starting   Ⓑ school ending
   Ⓒ a birthday   Ⓓ New Year's Day

3. These students are probably going to _____.

   Ⓐ a party   Ⓑ study
   Ⓒ play   Ⓓ watch television

4. This is most likely a _____ party.

   Ⓐ dog   Ⓑ holiday
   Ⓒ beach   Ⓓ surprise

5. Grayson is looking for his _____.

   Ⓐ dog   Ⓑ mom
   Ⓒ cat   Ⓓ sister

6. Allie is probably going _____.

   Ⓐ swimming   Ⓑ snow skiing
   Ⓒ to the beach   Ⓓ to school

Name _____ Date _____

Directions: Fill in the circle next to the sentence that is a fact.

7.
- Ⓐ The sun is a star.
- Ⓑ It is fun to learn about the sun.
- Ⓒ The moon is awesome.
- Ⓓ Stars tell really neat stories.

8.
- Ⓐ Dogs make great pets.
- Ⓑ Cats are the best indoor pets.
- Ⓒ People have all different kinds of pets.
- Ⓓ The best pet is a snake.

9.
- Ⓐ Scientists have really cool jobs.
- Ⓑ Pilots can fly airplanes or helicopters.
- Ⓒ Teachers are nice.
- Ⓓ The best job would be principal.

10.
- Ⓐ A train set would make a great gift for a child.
- Ⓑ A little girl would want a pony for her birthday.
- Ⓒ A boy would want a computer for his birthday.
- Ⓓ Each birthday you turn one year older.

Directions: Fill in the circle next to each sentence that is an opinion.

11.
- Ⓐ There are nine planets in our solar system.
- Ⓑ We live on the planet Earth.
- Ⓒ Mercury is the closest planet to the sun.
- Ⓓ Mars is the most interesting planet.

12.
- Ⓐ Playing football is fun.
- Ⓑ You get six points for a touchdown.
- Ⓒ You get one point for an extra point.
- Ⓓ You get three points for a field goal.

13.
- Ⓐ Math is a subject you learn in school.
- Ⓑ Math includes adding and subtracting.
- Ⓒ Math is the best subject.
- Ⓓ Calculators can help you with math.

14.
- Ⓐ Plants need air, sunlight, and water to live.
- Ⓑ Children need shelter, food, and water.
- Ⓒ Exercising is good for your body.
- Ⓓ Soccer is the best way to exercise.

Name _____ Date _____

Directions: Read each story. Fill in the circle next to the best answer for each question.

Grandma's House

I love going to my grandma's house. My family drives to see her every summer. She lives in Louisiana, and we live in Virginia. It takes us a long time to get to her house.

My grandma loves to cook. She makes delicious cornbread and vegetables. My favorite thing she makes is German chocolate cake. It is the best dessert in the world.

My cousins live across the street from my grandma. My brother, sister, and I play with our cousins all day. At night we read to each other and tell scary stories. Since our cousins are older than we are, they usually tell us the scariest stories.

I am lucky because I get to sleep with my grandma while we are at her house. She rubs my back and tells me a story every night. Sometimes I rub her back and tell her a story, too.

Everyone is sad when it is time to leave. I usually cry in the car on the way home because I miss my grandma. I really hate leaving her house. I can't wait until the next summer when I can go back.

1. This story is _____.
   Ⓐ nonfiction   Ⓑ poetry

2. My grandma is a great cook. I like her cake the best.
   In the sentence above, who is "her"?
   Ⓐ cousin   Ⓑ grandma
   Ⓒ sister   Ⓓ mother

3. How does the author feel when she leaves her grandma's house?
   Ⓐ sad   Ⓑ happy
   Ⓒ playful   Ⓓ angry

4. This story is mainly about _____.
   Ⓐ leaving Grandma's house
   Ⓑ visiting Grandma's house
   Ⓒ playing with cousins
   Ⓓ driving in the car with the family

Dear Mom and Dad,

I am having a great time at camp. I have met lots of new friends. One guy named Mark is in my cabin crew. He is also nine years old. We have a lot in common. He likes model cars and painting, just like I do!

My camp counselor is helping us learn how to paddle a canoe. We are also learning what to do if the canoe flips over. It is really hard! I am also learning new songs just for camp.

I hope you are having fun. Tell Haley hi for me and that she will have a great time next year when she is old enough to come to camp, too. Please give Hootie an extra treat from me, and tell him there are no dogs here, so I really miss him. I can't wait to see you next week.

Love,

Carson

1. Carson is _____ years old.
   Ⓐ twelve
   Ⓑ nine
   Ⓒ ten
   Ⓓ the story doesn't tell

2. Hootie is a _____.
   Ⓐ cat
   Ⓑ baby
   Ⓒ dog
   Ⓓ the story doesn't tell

3. Carson likes to _____.
   Ⓐ paint
   Ⓑ draw
   Ⓒ play outside
   Ⓓ swim

4. Carson's parents will pick him up from camp _____.
   Ⓐ in two weeks
   Ⓑ tomorrow
   Ⓒ next week
   Ⓓ in three days

Name   Date

Capitalization

Directions: Fill in the circle next to the word group that needs a capital letter.

Example:
- ● the boys
- Ⓑ went to the
- Ⓒ park last week.
- Ⓓ None

Look for the word in each sentence that needs to be capitalized.

Practice

1.
   - Ⓐ School starts Ⓑ next
   - Ⓒ wednesday. Ⓓ None

2.
   - Ⓐ Our class
   - Ⓑ has a party
   - Ⓒ on valentine's Day.
   - Ⓓ None

3.
   - Ⓐ Mr. johnson Ⓑ mailed the letter
   - Ⓒ yesterday. Ⓓ None

4.
   - Ⓐ i told
   - Ⓑ my mom to
   - Ⓒ pick me up at school.
   - Ⓓ None

5.
   - Ⓐ Susan and Ⓑ joey will
   - Ⓒ walk home. Ⓓ None

6.
   - Ⓐ Courtney Ⓑ lives on
   - Ⓒ taylor street. Ⓓ None

7.
   - Ⓐ We have
   - Ⓑ memorial day
   - Ⓒ off from school.
   - Ⓓ None

8.
   - Ⓐ Our first ball game
   - Ⓑ is at
   - Ⓒ cedarbluff elementary.
   - Ⓓ None

| Name | Date |

Capitalization

Directions: Fill in the circle next to the word in each sentence that should be capitalized.

Example: A. Let's go to the movies on tuesday.
  Ⓐ movies
  ● tuesday
  Ⓒ go

 You should capitalize the beginning of each sentence and proper nouns.

Practice

1. what time does the show end?
   Ⓐ show
   Ⓑ what
   Ⓒ time

2. I ordered the book from books-r-us.
   Ⓐ book
   Ⓑ books-r-us
   Ⓒ ordered

3. Meg lives on Highwater street.
   Ⓐ lives
   Ⓑ on
   Ⓒ street

4. mr. Jones is my spelling teacher.
   Ⓐ mr.
   Ⓑ teacher
   Ⓒ my

5. My math teacher is Mrs. anderson.
   Ⓐ math
   Ⓑ teacher
   Ⓒ anderson

6. peachtree Gym closes at 7:00.
   Ⓐ closes
   Ⓑ peachtree
   Ⓒ at

7. Turn right on Emerson lane.
   Ⓐ right
   Ⓑ on
   Ⓒ lane

8. the television show comes on tonight.
   Ⓐ television
   Ⓑ the
   Ⓒ tonight

Test Prep Connection—Grade 2—RBP0857   www.summerbridgeactivities.com

Name   Date

Directions: Fill in the circle next to the sentence that is correct.

9.
- Ⓐ i am eight years old.
- Ⓑ My birthday is in july.
- Ⓒ mark is six years old.
- Ⓓ His birthday is in May.

10.
- Ⓐ I was born in memphis, Tennessee.
- Ⓑ My mother was born in Mississippi.
- Ⓒ my father was born in st. Louis.
- Ⓓ Now we live in virginia.

11.
- Ⓐ My best friend is Laura.
- Ⓑ she is in my class.
- Ⓒ We both live on hilton street.
- Ⓓ we like the same things.

12.
- Ⓐ I met Julie at the park tuesday.
- Ⓑ Saturday is my favorite day of the week.
- Ⓒ i like to watch cartoons on Saturday.
- Ⓓ my mom likes Fridays.

Directions: Look at the blanks in the envelope. Fill in the circle next to the correct answer for each blank.

13.
- Ⓐ Jill rogers
- Ⓑ jill rogers
- Ⓒ Jill Rogers
- Ⓓ jill Rogers

14.
- Ⓐ richmond, va 23219
- Ⓑ Richmond, va 23219
- Ⓒ richmond, VA 23219
- Ⓓ Richmond, VA 23219

15.
- Ⓐ 678 Cottage Lane
- Ⓑ 678 cottage Lane
- Ⓒ 678 Cottage lane
- Ⓓ 678 cottage lane

Name _____ Date _____

Punctuation

Directions: Look at each sentence carefully. Fill in the circle next to the correct punctuation for each sentence.

Examples:

A. Where are we going
- Ⓐ .
- Ⓑ !
- ● ?
- Ⓓ None

B. She is wearing a blue shirt
- ● .
- Ⓑ !
- Ⓒ ?
- Ⓓ None

 Read each sentence carefully. Decide if it is a question, statement, or exclamation.

Practice

1. The cat is stuck in the tree
   - Ⓐ .
   - Ⓑ !
   - Ⓒ ?
   - Ⓓ None

2. What time does the train leave
   - Ⓐ .
   - Ⓑ !
   - Ⓒ ?
   - Ⓓ None

3. How old is the puppy
   - Ⓐ .
   - Ⓑ !
   - Ⓒ ?
   - Ⓓ None

4. The book had a very sad ending
   - Ⓐ .
   - Ⓑ !
   - Ⓒ ?
   - Ⓓ None

5. Please move the dishes
   - Ⓐ .
   - Ⓑ !
   - Ⓒ ?
   - Ⓓ None

6. Watch out for the wave
   - Ⓐ .
   - Ⓑ !
   - Ⓒ ?
   - Ⓓ None

Name _____   Date _____

Punctuation

Directions: Fill in the circle next to the sentence that is punctuated correctly.

Examples:

A.
- ● Watch out for the car!
- Ⓑ Where are you going.
- Ⓒ Let's ride the boat?

B.
- Ⓐ Look at the seagulls?
- ● Why did she move?
- Ⓒ How is your mom.

 Remember to look for the sentence that is punctuated correctly.

Practice

1.
- Ⓐ Take your hat scarf and mittens.
- Ⓑ Did you remember your socks?
- Ⓒ How much longer will this take.

2.
- Ⓐ The ceiling is painted yellow!
- Ⓑ Watch out for the swing!
- Ⓒ What is your cousin's name!

3.
- Ⓐ Give me the toy.
- Ⓑ Go under the bridge?
- Ⓒ Turn left at the light!

4.
- Ⓐ I bought bread, yogurt, and turkey at the store.
- Ⓑ I saw Mickey buy ice cream?
- Ⓒ Nan bought juice and hot dogs!

Directions: Fill in the circle next to the group of words that are correctly punctuated.

5.
- Ⓐ Love Lilly
- Ⓑ Love, Lilly
- Ⓒ Love. Lilly

6.
- Ⓐ New Orleans, Louisiana
- Ⓑ New Orleans. Louisiana
- Ⓒ New Orleans Louisiana

7.
- Ⓐ milk, juice, and bread
- Ⓑ milk juice and bread
- Ⓒ milk. juice. and bread.

8.
- Ⓐ Dear Mom
- Ⓑ Dear. Mom
- Ⓒ Dear Mom,

Name   Date

Punctuation

Directions: Fill in the circle next to the part of the story that is missing punctuation.

Examples:

A.
- Ⓐ We went to the zoo
- ● on a field trip
- Ⓒ It was a lot of fun.

B.
- Ⓐ I can meet you
- Ⓑ at Piedmont Park
- ● at noon

 Look for the part of the story that is missing punctuation.

Practice

1.
- Ⓐ Barbara called
- Ⓑ four times yesterday.
- Ⓒ Does she need something

2.
- Ⓐ Millie ran five laps in the
- Ⓑ relay race yesterday
- Ⓒ She is really fast.

3.
- Ⓐ My grandparents bought a
- Ⓑ painting in Italy. They go
- Ⓒ there every summer

4.
- Ⓐ Football is my favorite sport
- Ⓑ I used to play with my dad.
- Ⓒ What is your favorite team?

5.
- Ⓐ I love to celebrate birthdays.
- Ⓑ I was born on March 19 1997
- Ⓒ in Knoxville, Tennessee.

6.
- Ⓐ When I grow up, I want to
- Ⓑ be a movie star and live in
- Ⓒ Hollywood California.

Name   Date

Capitalization and Punctuation

Directions: Fill in the circle next to the sentence or phrase that is correct.

Examples: A. The party is _____.
- Ⓐ september 3, 2004
- ● September 3, 2004
- Ⓒ September 3 2004
- Ⓓ september 3, 2003

B.
- Ⓐ mr. Davis is my neighbor.
- ● He walks my dog for me.
- Ⓒ i walk his dog too.
- Ⓓ His dog's name is Lou

 Remember to look for <u>correct</u> capitalization and punctuation.

Practice

1.
- Ⓐ Mom says we have to clean house.
- Ⓑ our grandparents came to visit.
- Ⓒ They live in charleston, SC.
- Ⓓ i love it when they visit.

2.
- Ⓐ we go to charlotte for Thanksgiving.
- Ⓑ Charlotte is the largest city in North Carolina.
- Ⓒ My moms sister lives there
- Ⓓ She has two kids, marge and tom.

3.
- Ⓐ Dear kate,
- Ⓑ I'm having a great time in Hawaii.
- Ⓒ I wish you were here?
- Ⓓ love, andrea

4.
- Ⓐ Directions to my house are easy
- Ⓑ follow old ivy through stop light.
- Ⓒ Turn left on Juniper Street.
- Ⓓ I live in the second house on the right

5.
- Ⓐ We went to pet aid to buy medicine for the dog.
- Ⓑ he has been sick for three days.
- Ⓒ Pet Aid is on cactus boulevard.
- Ⓓ Do you know what is wrong with my dog?

6.
- Ⓐ My favorite mall is Lakefront Mall.
- Ⓑ i go there with my sister.
- Ⓒ My dad lets her take the car out once a week?
- Ⓓ She is lots older that I am

| Name | Date |

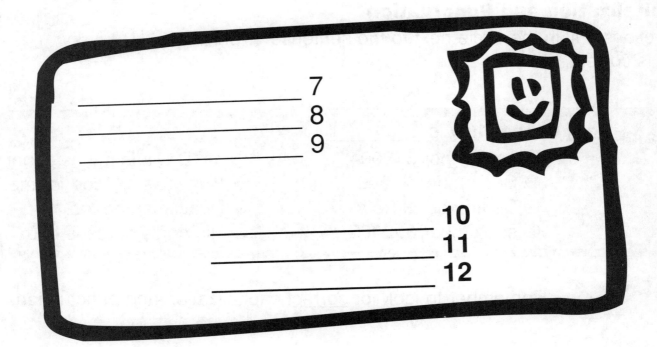

Directions: For problems 7–15, look at the numbered blanks on the envelope and letter. Fill in the circle next to the correct answer for each number.

7.
- Ⓐ carrie Moore
- Ⓑ Carrie Moore
- Ⓒ Carrie moore

8.
- Ⓐ 533 Minnie Road
- Ⓑ 533 minnie rd
- Ⓒ 533 Minnie road

9.
- Ⓐ Austin Texas 78705
- Ⓑ Austin. Texas
- Ⓒ Austin, Texas 78705

10.
- Ⓐ Sarah Taylor
- Ⓑ sarah, Taylor
- Ⓒ Sarah taylor

11.
- Ⓐ 7128 longbranch lane
- Ⓑ 7128 Longbranch lane
- Ⓒ 7128 Longbranch Lane

12.
- Ⓐ Vicksburg, MS 39180
- Ⓑ vicksburg, ms 39180
- Ⓒ Vicksburg, ms 39180

Name _____ Date _____

Directions: Fill in the circle next to the answer that shows the correct punctuation and capitalization for the sentences.

13.

14.

    I am having a great time at Grandma's house. We play games and eat ice cream every night. I even get to watch cartoons every morning. During the day we go swimming and to the park. I wish you were here with us. I miss you, and so does Grandma.

15.

16. What time will you pick me up i will wait for you by the curb.
  Ⓐ up? I
  Ⓑ up! I
  Ⓒ up. i
  Ⓓ up. I

13.
  Ⓐ June 19, 2004
  Ⓑ June 19 2004
  Ⓒ june 19, 2004
  Ⓓ June 19. 2004

17. Did you see the movie it was really good.
  Ⓐ movie. It
  Ⓑ movie. it
  Ⓒ movie? It
  Ⓓ movie! It

14.
  Ⓐ dear mom
  Ⓑ Dear Mom.
  Ⓒ Dear Mom,
  Ⓓ Dear. Mom.

18. My favorite food is pizza what's your favorite food?
  Ⓐ pizza. what's
  Ⓑ pizza? What's
  Ⓒ pizza. What's
  Ⓓ pizza? what's

15.
  Ⓐ Love, allen
  Ⓑ Love, Allen
  Ⓒ love, allen
  Ⓓ love, Allen

Name _____ Date _____

Spelling

Directions: Fill in the circle next to the word that fits in the blank and is spelled correctly.

Examples:
A. The dog had a _____ for lunch.
  Ⓐ bon   ● bone
  Ⓒ boan   Ⓓ bonn

B. The show starts at _____ o'clock.
  Ⓐ fyve   Ⓑ fiev
  ● five   Ⓓ fiv

 Eliminate words you know are wrong.

Practice

1. The directory has everyone's phone number and _____.
   Ⓐ adres
   Ⓑ addres
   Ⓒ address
   Ⓓ adress

2. My mother went _____ with her sister.
   Ⓐ shop
   Ⓑ shoping
   Ⓒ shoppin
   Ⓓ shopping

3. Tomorrow is Julie's _____.
   Ⓐ birthdae
   Ⓑ birthda
   Ⓒ birthday
   Ⓓ birth day

4. Lucy used her favorite color to draw the _____.
   Ⓐ howse
   Ⓑ house
   Ⓒ hose
   Ⓓ howes

| Name | Date |

5. My _____ feeds my cat when I am on vacation.

Ⓐ neighbor
Ⓑ neaybor
Ⓒ neghbor
Ⓓ naybor

6. I _____ in line for fifteen minutes.

Ⓐ wayted
Ⓑ wated
Ⓒ waeted
Ⓓ waited

7. Firefighters and police officers _____ hats.

Ⓐ wear
Ⓑ where
Ⓒ were
Ⓓ ware

8. I'll call Joey to _____ us for dinner.

Ⓐ mete
Ⓑ met
Ⓒ meet
Ⓓ meat

9. Mark keeps his _____ at the dock.

Ⓐ bote
Ⓑ boat
Ⓒ bot
Ⓓ boet

10. The _____ book comes out Friday.

Ⓐ new
Ⓑ neew
Ⓒ noo
Ⓓ newe

Name _____ Date _____

Spelling

Directions: Fill in the circle next to the word that is <u>not</u> spelled correctly.

Examples:

A.
● yelow
Ⓑ rake
Ⓒ hello

B.
Ⓐ under
Ⓑ sea
● fis

Remember, you are looking for the words that are <u>not</u> spelled correctly.

Practice

1.
Ⓐ target   Ⓑ stor   Ⓒ cream

2.
Ⓐ states   Ⓑ flight   Ⓒ trep

3.
Ⓐ uze   Ⓑ cry   Ⓒ make

4.
Ⓐ lake   Ⓑ river   Ⓒ yurn

5.
Ⓐ truck   Ⓑ duk   Ⓒ dive

6.
Ⓐ write   Ⓑ bok   Ⓒ stand

7.
Ⓐ boxes   Ⓑ wash   Ⓒ juge

8.
Ⓐ pik   Ⓑ peak   Ⓒ puddle

9.
Ⓐ mud   Ⓑ throw   Ⓒ tric

10.
Ⓐ tabl   Ⓑ even   Ⓒ week

Name   Date

Spelling

Directions: Fill in the circle next to the word that is spelled correctly.

Examples:

A.
- ● green
- Ⓑ gren
- Ⓒ grene

B.
- ● eight
- Ⓑ hite
- Ⓒ fiht

Remember this time you are looking for the word that is spelled correctly.

Practice

1. Ⓐ turcey Ⓑ thanks Ⓒ trane

2. Ⓐ like Ⓑ rit Ⓒ forgoten

3. Ⓐ wach Ⓑ time Ⓒ clok

4. Ⓐ fuld Ⓑ viser Ⓒ shine

5. Ⓐ cheap Ⓑ cherp Ⓒ chang

6. Ⓐ trep Ⓑ eys Ⓒ crash

7. Ⓐ skool Ⓑ learn Ⓒ teash

8. Ⓐ color Ⓑ fod Ⓒ staf

9. Ⓐ picshure Ⓑ pour Ⓒ drinke

10. Ⓐ fram Ⓑ grat Ⓒ velvet

| Name | Date |

Spelling

Directions: Fill in the circle next to the word that is not spelled correctly in each sentence.

Examples:

A. Did you git the idea from a friend?
- ● git
- Ⓑ idea
- Ⓒ friend

B. What tyme are you leaving?
- ● tyme
- Ⓑ are
- Ⓒ leaving

 You are looking for the word that is misspelled.

Practice

1. I read the book for clas.
   - Ⓐ read
   - Ⓑ book
   - Ⓒ clas

2. My familie went to the mountains for vacation.
   - Ⓐ familie
   - Ⓑ mountains
   - Ⓒ vacation

3. I got lots of presints on my birthday.
   - Ⓐ lots
   - Ⓑ presints
   - Ⓒ birthday

4. School is over in Maye.
   - Ⓐ School
   - Ⓑ over
   - Ⓒ Maye

Name _____   Date _____

5. My class went hiking by the rever.

Ⓐ class
Ⓑ hiking
Ⓒ rever

6. The bad guys alwaiys go to jail.

Ⓐ bad
Ⓑ alwaiys
Ⓒ jail

7. I saw him at the markit on Sunday.

Ⓐ him
Ⓑ markit
Ⓒ Sunday

8. The hoarse lives in the stable.

Ⓐ hoarse
Ⓑ lives
Ⓒ stable

9. We knead a spiral notebook for school.

Ⓐ knead
Ⓑ spiral
Ⓒ school

10. I bought bread at the grocery stor.

Ⓐ bought
Ⓑ bread
Ⓒ stor

Name _____ Date _____

Sample Test

Directions: Fill in the circle next to the group of words that needs a capital.

1.
   - Ⓐ When did
   - Ⓑ joe arrive
   - Ⓒ at the party?
   - Ⓓ None

2.
   - Ⓐ most children
   - Ⓑ like
   - Ⓒ macaroni and cheese.
   - Ⓓ None

3.
   - Ⓐ Jane's birthday
   - Ⓑ is in
   - Ⓒ november.
   - Ⓓ None

4.
   - Ⓐ We moved to
   - Ⓑ spring street
   - Ⓒ last fall.
   - Ⓓ None

5.
   - Ⓐ Judge lawson
   - Ⓑ handled
   - Ⓒ the case.
   - Ⓓ None

Directions: Fill in the circle next to the word in each sentence that needs to be capitalized.

6. brett and I are good friends.
   - Ⓐ brett   Ⓑ are
   - Ⓒ good   Ⓓ friends

7. Poppy went to europe last year.
   - Ⓐ went   Ⓑ europe
   - Ⓒ last   Ⓓ year

8. Karen and I went to the knoxville Zoo.
   - Ⓐ went   Ⓑ to
   - Ⓒ the   Ⓓ knoxville

9. dara's new car is gray.
   - Ⓐ dara's Ⓑ new
   - Ⓒ car   Ⓓ gray

10. The candle came from a store at lakeshore Mall.
- Ⓐ candle
- Ⓑ from
- Ⓒ store
- Ⓓ lakeshore

11. I take piano lessons from mrs. Ragland.
- Ⓐ piano
- Ⓑ lessons
- Ⓒ from
- Ⓓ mrs.

Directions: Fill in the circle next to the sentence that is punctuated correctly.

12.
- Ⓐ Farmers grow corn beans and tomatoes on the farm.
- Ⓑ Lisa likes pizza, tacos, and hamburgers.
- Ⓒ Movie popcorn is my favorite?

13.
- Ⓐ What time do we need to be at the airport?
- Ⓑ We need to be at the airport at 8:00
- Ⓒ The flight, leaves at 9:00!

14.
- Ⓐ The car broke down in Jackson Mississippi.
- Ⓑ It took two days to get it fixed.
- Ⓒ We finally got home on Tuesday?

Directions: Fill in the circle next to the group of words that are correctly punctuated.

15.
- Ⓐ Jeff, Steve, and Andrew
- Ⓑ Jeff Steve and Andrew
- Ⓒ Jeff. Steve. And Andrew.

16.
- Ⓐ Dear Kyle?
- Ⓑ Dear Kyle,
- Ⓒ Dear Kyle.

17.
- Ⓐ Salt Lake City. Utah
- Ⓑ Salt Lake City Utah
- Ⓒ Salt Lake City, Utah

Directions: Fill in the circle next to the sentence or phrase that is correct. Look for correct capitalization and punctuation.

18. We leave for the trip on _____.
    Ⓐ october 5, 2004
    Ⓑ October 5 2004
    Ⓒ October 5, 2004
    Ⓓ October 5. 2004

19.
    Ⓐ Lucy moved to Hawaii last year.
    Ⓑ I really want to go visit?
    Ⓒ It takes a long time to fly to hawaii.
    Ⓓ maybe I can go visit lucy soon

20.
    Ⓐ We went hiking in the mountains in tennessee.
    Ⓑ It took us one hour to hike one trail?
    Ⓒ We took a snack to eat on the way.
    Ⓓ We also took lots of water,

21.
    Ⓐ We went to graceland on a field trip.
    Ⓑ Graceland is the home of Elvis Presley.
    Ⓒ he was a famous singer.
    Ⓓ Graceland is in memphis, tennessee.

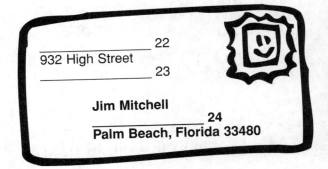

22.
    Ⓐ al Sanders
    Ⓑ Al Sanders
    Ⓒ Al sanders

23.
    Ⓐ raleigh, nc 27601
    Ⓑ Raleigh, nc 27601
    Ⓒ Raleigh, NC 27601

24.
    Ⓐ 699 Court Street
    Ⓑ 699 court street
    Ⓒ 699 court Street

Name _____ Date _____

Directions: Fill in the circle next to the word that is spelled correctly.

25.
- Ⓐ lake
- Ⓑ lak
- Ⓒ layk

26.
- Ⓐ polise
- Ⓑ police
- Ⓒ polic

27.
- Ⓐ copy
- Ⓑ hav
- Ⓒ treet

28.
- Ⓐ poni
- Ⓑ clowd
- Ⓒ pie

29.
- Ⓐ cute
- Ⓑ pla
- Ⓒ resess

Directions: Fill in the circle next to the word that fits in the blank and is spelled correctly.

30. The _____ plays all day.
- Ⓐ cheld
- Ⓑ kide
- Ⓒ child

31. The _____ went over the creek.
- Ⓐ brige
- Ⓑ bridge
- Ⓒ campe

32. Close the _____ on the window.
- Ⓐ kurtan
- Ⓑ curtan
- Ⓒ curtain

33. The flag is red, _____, and blue.
- Ⓐ white
- Ⓑ wite
- Ⓒ wyte

| Name | Date |

Usage

Directions: Read each sentence carefully. Fill in the circle next to the word or phrase that should go in the blank or substitute for the underlined part.

Examples:

A. He _____ those pants Tuesday.
- Ⓐ were
- Ⓑ where
- Ⓒ wores
- ● wore

B. Sue had <u>John's</u> hat the whole time.
- Ⓐ her
- ● his
- Ⓒ it's
- Ⓓ him

Read each sentence carefully. Remember, your first answer is usually the right answer.

Practice

1. When did <u>Mack</u> get here?
   - Ⓐ her
   - Ⓑ his
   - Ⓒ he
   - Ⓓ him

2. Jill is the _____ person I know.
   - Ⓐ nice
   - Ⓑ nicer
   - Ⓒ more nicest
   - Ⓓ nicest

3. June is the best month because <u>June</u> is hot.
   - Ⓐ they
   - Ⓑ it
   - Ⓒ all
   - Ⓓ we'll

4. My sister is the _____ runner in the school.
   - Ⓐ fast
   - Ⓑ faster
   - Ⓒ most fast
   - Ⓓ fastest

5. I like <u>Sarah's</u> brother.
   - Ⓐ her
   - Ⓑ shes
   - Ⓒ him
   - Ⓓ hers

6. Jake is very _____ for a puppy.
   - Ⓐ excited
   - Ⓑ excitement
   - Ⓒ exciting
   - Ⓓ excite

Name _____   Date _____

7. The teacher took <u>Sean and me</u> to the office.
   Ⓐ us
   Ⓑ me
   Ⓒ I
   Ⓓ it

8. Is the snail _____ than the turtle?
   Ⓐ slowest
   Ⓑ more slow
   Ⓒ slow
   Ⓓ slower

9. When the phone rings, <u>the phone</u> plays a song.
   Ⓐ they
   Ⓑ it
   Ⓒ its
   Ⓓ us

10. The phone _____ four times yesterday.
    Ⓐ rings
    Ⓑ rang
    Ⓒ ring
    Ⓓ rangs

11. Shelly _____ the vase with the baseball.
    Ⓐ broke
    Ⓑ broken
    Ⓒ broked
    Ⓓ brokes

12. We _____ the treasure chest in the sand.
    Ⓐ finds
    Ⓑ finded
    Ⓒ found
    Ⓓ finder

13. You could see the shooting star as <u>the shooting star</u> fell.
    Ⓐ she
    Ⓑ he
    Ⓒ they
    Ⓓ it

14. Bradley wants to play with <u>Andrew</u> ten more minutes.
    Ⓐ his
    Ⓑ him
    Ⓒ she
    Ⓓ he

Name _____ Date _____

Usage

Directions: Read each sentence. Fill in the circle next to the part of the sentence that is not correct.

Language

Examples:

A.
● Me and my sister
Ⓑ love to
Ⓒ ride horses.

B.
● I looks
Ⓑ under the
Ⓒ chair for the book.

You are looking for the part of the sentence that is **not** correct.

Practice

1.
Ⓐ What time
Ⓑ is her
Ⓒ playing in the game?

2.
Ⓐ How much money
Ⓑ does they
Ⓒ have?

3.
Ⓐ When is they
Ⓑ going to study
Ⓒ Native Americans?

4.
Ⓐ Abby
Ⓑ and me
Ⓒ can skip.

5.
Ⓐ Daddy and us
Ⓑ went fishing
Ⓒ in the ocean.

6.
Ⓐ My mom
Ⓑ took
Ⓒ we to the zoo.

GO ON

7.
- Ⓐ Did she
- Ⓑ meet he
- Ⓒ at the game?

8.
- Ⓐ You'll read
- Ⓑ that book when
- Ⓒ you in fifth grade.

9.
- Ⓐ Who won the
- Ⓑ tennis match?
- Ⓒ She think Marty did.

10.
- Ⓐ I like
- Ⓑ you haircut.
- Ⓒ It looks good.

11.
- Ⓐ We had a substitute
- Ⓑ today. She name
- Ⓒ was Mrs. Wilkinson.

12.
- Ⓐ Us school
- Ⓑ was the
- Ⓒ fastest on the track.

13.
- Ⓐ I favorite
- Ⓑ season
- Ⓒ is spring.

14.
- Ⓐ My best
- Ⓑ subject are
- Ⓒ reading.

15.
- Ⓐ I were
- Ⓑ born in
- Ⓒ July.

16.
- Ⓐ We goes
- Ⓑ to bed
- Ⓒ at 8:00.

| Name | Date |

Sentences

Directions: Look at the sentences below. Fill in the circle next to the phrase that correctly completes each sentence.

Examples:
A. The movie _____.
- Ⓐ is about
- Ⓑ begins
- ● is on tonight
- Ⓓ has

B. We went _____.
- Ⓐ yesterday's
- Ⓑ to the
- Ⓒ the car
- ● to the park

Remember to fill in the circle next to the phrase that will make the sentence complete. A sentence is a complete thought.

Practice

1. The newspaper _____.
   - Ⓐ is overnight
   - Ⓑ was delivered at noon
   - Ⓒ at midnight
   - Ⓓ with sports

2. Wear old clothes _____.
   - Ⓐ to play in the park
   - Ⓑ playing
   - Ⓒ park
   - Ⓓ and shoes to the

3. _____ take the test on Monday.
   - Ⓐ The boy
   - Ⓑ The students will
   - Ⓒ Child
   - Ⓓ Teachers can do

4. _____ ate dinner together.
   - Ⓐ Family
   - Ⓑ Friends
   - Ⓒ The family
   - Ⓓ I

Name _____ Date _____

5. The sun _____.
   Ⓐ shiny
   Ⓑ was bright
   Ⓒ hot
   Ⓓ covered by clouds

6. We moved _____.
   Ⓐ new house
   Ⓑ one hour
   Ⓒ last year
   Ⓓ tomorrow

7. The children _____.
   Ⓐ play well together
   Ⓑ watching
   Ⓒ screamed on the
   Ⓓ rolled to

8. Look _____.
   Ⓐ over
   Ⓑ under the chair
   Ⓒ on the
   Ⓓ behind our

9. The presents _____.
   Ⓐ open
   Ⓑ hid under
   Ⓒ were opened
   Ⓓ wrapped

10. We brought _____.
    Ⓐ cat to our house
    Ⓑ bunnies from
    Ⓒ a snake's
    Ⓓ the dog home

11. Tennis _____.
    Ⓐ are good
    Ⓑ is good exercise
    Ⓒ really fun
    Ⓓ need a ball

12. I read _____.
    Ⓐ hour
    Ⓑ good book
    Ⓒ to my dad
    Ⓓ sisters

| Name | Date |

Directions: Fill in the circle next to the complete sentence.

13.
- Ⓐ Fruit is apple.
- Ⓑ Fruit is good for you.
- Ⓒ Make you grow strong.
- Ⓓ And drink milk.

14.
- Ⓐ We bought toy.
- Ⓑ A toy fun.
- Ⓒ Tom likes to play.
- Ⓓ He play.

15.
- Ⓐ Music play.
- Ⓑ Joe and the guitar.
- Ⓒ Amy got instrument.
- Ⓓ Jill plays the piano.

16.
- Ⓐ Warm blankets in box.
- Ⓑ Quilts are in the chest.
- Ⓒ Comforter is bed.
- Ⓓ The sheets and cover.

17.
- Ⓐ The movie began at noon.
- Ⓑ Show film yesterday.
- Ⓒ Turn television.
- Ⓓ The show started and.

18.
- Ⓐ Shirt and shoes.
- Ⓑ The shirt is yellow.
- Ⓒ The shoes can until.
- Ⓓ Clothes are what you.

19.
- Ⓐ Put the flowers down.
- Ⓑ Flowers grow in.
- Ⓒ Garden is there.
- Ⓓ The path is over.

20.
- Ⓐ Washing laundry.
- Ⓑ Shirt is dirty.
- Ⓒ The clothes are clean.
- Ⓓ Muddy socks.

Directions: Fill in the circle next to the phrase that is not part of a complete sentence.

21.
- Ⓐ The concert will start
- Ⓑ at 8:00 tomorrow.
- Ⓒ Going with mother.

22.
- Ⓐ Nail polish and lipstick.
- Ⓑ Judy bought
- Ⓒ candy at the store.

23.
- Ⓐ When you leave.
- Ⓑ Will you please
- Ⓒ take out the trash?

24.
- Ⓐ There are fifty
- Ⓑ states in the U.S.A.
- Ⓒ Live from Georgia.

25.
- Ⓐ My favorite food.
- Ⓑ Dad likes pizza
- Ⓒ the best.

26.
- Ⓐ Dan is moving to
- Ⓑ New Mexico.
- Ⓒ Is new.

27.
- Ⓐ When you?
- Ⓑ When did
- Ⓒ you finish?

28.
- Ⓐ In music class
- Ⓑ we like to sing.
- Ⓒ Country music.

29.
- Ⓐ What time.
- Ⓑ The wedding is
- Ⓒ in New Orleans.

30.
- Ⓐ The horse.
- Ⓑ Horses live
- Ⓒ on farms.

Name _____ Date _____

Paragraphs

Directions: Fill in the circle next to the sentence that best fits in the paragraph.

Examples: A. There are all different types of music. _____ What is your favorite type of music?
● Some people like classical music, while others like jazz.
Ⓑ Some people listen to the radio.
Ⓒ Sometimes I listen to music on television.
Ⓓ I like Elvis Presley.

 Remember to choose the sentence that makes the most sense in each paragraph.

Practice

1. Baseball is a sport mainly played in the summer months. I play second base on the Braves. _____

   Ⓐ I like football.
   Ⓑ I really enjoy playing baseball.
   Ⓒ Basketball is cool, too.
   Ⓓ Playing sports is fun.

2. My sister got her driving permit last week. _____ I am so glad my sister has her driving permit.

   Ⓐ My mother thinks she should drive me to school every day.
   Ⓑ My sister is in tenth grade.
   Ⓒ My brother is twelve.
   Ⓓ My dad likes to fish.

3. _____ Some fish are good to cook and eat. Other fish make good pets.

   Ⓐ Dogs make good pets.
   Ⓑ There are lots of different kinds of fish.
   Ⓒ Cats like to eat fish.
   Ⓓ There are lots of different kinds of pets.

Name _____ Date _____

4. Emily loves to dance. _____ Emily is an excellent dancer.

   Ⓐ She likes to play the piano.
   Ⓑ She has taken dance lessons for five years.
   Ⓒ She eats lots of ice cream.
   Ⓓ She is ten years old.

5. The children play outside until 4:30. Then they come inside to complete their homework. _____

   Ⓐ They eat dinner at 6:30 p.m.
   Ⓑ The children wake up each day at 7:00 a.m.
   Ⓒ The children ride the school bus to school.
   Ⓓ The dog's name is Buzz.

6. _____ The best float was by the local high school seniors. The band played our fight song while they marched.

   Ⓐ The party will begin at 7:30 p.m.
   Ⓑ The band marched all day.
   Ⓒ The homecoming parade started on High Street.
   Ⓓ We went to the movies last night.

7. The children planted the flowers in the garden. _____ Then they picked them for their teacher.

   Ⓐ The flowers ate lunch every day.
   Ⓑ They buried them in the ground.
   Ⓒ The neighbors cut the flowers.
   Ⓓ They watered the flowers each day.

8. The boy drew a picture of a lake. _____ He drew people at the campground.

   Ⓐ He likes to go camping.
   Ⓑ He gave the picture to his dad.
   Ⓒ He drew a campground by the lake.
   Ⓓ He drew trees and bushes by the road.

9. _____ They found an anthill by the fence. They also found old toys in the sandbox.

   Ⓐ The boys went exploring in the backyard.
   Ⓑ The boys played inside all day.
   Ⓒ The boys watched a movie.
   Ⓓ The boys ate sandwiches for lunch.

GO ON

Name _____ Date _____

Directions: Read each sentence. Decide if it is a beginning sentence in a paragraph or an ending sentence in a paragraph. Fill in the circle next to the correct answer.

10. You will not believe what happened to me last year.
    Ⓐ beginning
    Ⓑ ending

11. That's what I did over summer vacation.
    Ⓐ beginning
    Ⓑ ending

12. I once saw a dolphin at the beach.
    Ⓐ beginning
    Ⓑ ending

13. The four friends had a great time camping together.
    Ⓐ beginning
    Ⓑ ending

14. Listen to an amazing story.
    Ⓐ beginning
    Ⓑ ending

15. So we had a great snow day!
    Ⓐ beginning
    Ⓑ ending

16. The ice finally melted in May.
    Ⓐ beginning
    Ⓑ ending

17. Have you ever heard a story quite like that one?
    Ⓐ beginning
    Ⓑ ending

Steven is going to write a letter to his aunt about his new puppy.

18. What should Steven do before he writes his letter?

   Ⓐ draw a picture
   Ⓑ write some things down about his weekend
   Ⓒ write some things down about his puppy

19. What should the letter to Steven's aunt be about?

   Ⓐ his birthday party
   Ⓑ his new puppy
   Ⓒ his new school

June 17, 2004
Dear Aunt Elaine,

I got a new puppy yesterday. I got him at the Humane Society. My mom and dad took me. I named him Mack. I am eight years old. He is really sweet and really smart. I can't wait until you can meet him.

Love,
Steven

20. Which sentence does not belong in this paragraph?

   Ⓐ I got a new puppy yesterday.
   Ⓑ I am eight years old.
   Ⓒ He is really sweet and really smart.

21. Which sentence does belong in this paragraph?

   Ⓐ Mack is ten weeks old.
   Ⓑ I ate tacos for lunch.
   Ⓒ My birthday is in April.

Name Date

Directions: Fill in the circle next to the best title for each paragraph.

22. A paragraph about different types of pets.
    Ⓐ A Pet for Everyone
    Ⓑ Food for Pets
    Ⓒ Naming Your Pet

23. A paragraph about going to Hawaii on vacation.
    Ⓐ Snowboarding
    Ⓑ My Hawaiian Vacation
    Ⓒ Driving Rules

24. A paragraph about living in the country.
    Ⓐ City Life
    Ⓑ Country Life
    Ⓒ Life at the Beach

25. A paragraph about being the new kid at school.
    Ⓐ Growing Up in a Small Town
    Ⓑ The Lunchroom
    Ⓒ The New Kid at School

26. A paragraph about alligators.
    Ⓐ How to Wrap a Present
    Ⓑ Alligators
    Ⓒ Animals that Live in Swamps

27. A paragraph about learning to play the piano.
    Ⓐ History of the Piano
    Ⓑ Different Kinds of Instruments
    Ⓒ Piano Lessons

28. A paragraph about a person's favorite things to eat.
    Ⓐ My Favorite Foods
    Ⓑ Types of Desserts
    Ⓒ Foods from around the World

Study Skills

Directions: Fill in the circle next to the best answer for each question.

Table of Contents

History of Soccer 1
Countries That Play Soccer 7
Great Soccer Players . . 12
Rules of Soccer 19

1. On what page would you find out about different countries that play soccer?
   - Ⓐ 1
   - Ⓑ 7
   - Ⓒ 19

2. How many chapters are in this book?
   - Ⓐ 2
   - Ⓑ 3
   - Ⓒ 4

3. What is on page 12?
   - Ⓐ History of Soccer
   - Ⓑ Great Soccer Players
   - Ⓒ Rules of Soccer

Table of Contents

What a Spy Does 1
Spy Tools. 13
Codes and Secret Messages 16
Spy Clothing. 23

4. How many chapters are in this book?
   - Ⓐ 3
   - Ⓑ 5
   - Ⓒ 4

5. What is the most likely title for this book?
   - Ⓐ Foods That Spies Eat
   - Ⓑ Superheroes
   - Ⓒ How to Be a Spy

6. On what page would you find out about how to decode messages?
   - Ⓐ 13
   - Ⓑ 16
   - Ⓒ 1

spade —	a utensil with a blade for digging: I dug a hole for the plant with my spade.
spectacular —	impressive or sensational: The fireworks were spectacular after the ball game.
splash —	to scatter a fluid: The baby likes to splash in the bathtub.
spoon —	a utensil used for eating: Use your spoon to eat your cereal.

7. What is the last word defined on this page?
   Ⓐ spoon
   Ⓑ spread
   Ⓒ cereal

8. What would you use as an eating utensil?
   Ⓐ spade
   Ⓑ spoon
   Ⓒ splash

9. What word would you use in this sentence?
   The costumes in the show were absolutely ____.
   Ⓐ spectacular
   Ⓑ nice
   Ⓒ spoon

10. How many words are defined on this page?
    Ⓐ 2
    Ⓑ 3
    Ⓒ 4

11. What word would you use in this sentence?
    I used a ____ in the dirt.
    Ⓐ spoon
    Ⓑ spade
    Ⓒ spectacular

12. What word would you use in this sentence?
    The waves made a huge ____ when they hit the beach.
    Ⓐ spectacular
    Ⓑ splash
    Ⓒ huge

fan — a device used to cool the air

rake — a tool used to gather leaves on the ground

sundial — a type of clock people used many years ago to tell time

violin — a type of instrument used to make music

13. Who would most likely use a violin?
- Ⓐ a pilot
- Ⓑ a musician
- Ⓒ a doctor

14. When would you most likely use a fan?
- Ⓐ when it is snowing
- Ⓑ when it is hot
- Ⓒ when it is cold

15. Where would you most likely use a rake?
- Ⓐ in a backyard with trees
- Ⓑ on a beach with sand
- Ⓒ in a bedroom with floors

16. When would you most likely use a sundial?
- Ⓐ when it is dark and you need to see better
- Ⓑ when you don't know what time it is
- Ⓒ when you're cold and want to get warm

17. Which item would you use to play songs?
- Ⓐ a violin
- Ⓑ a sundial
- Ⓒ a rake

| Name | Date |

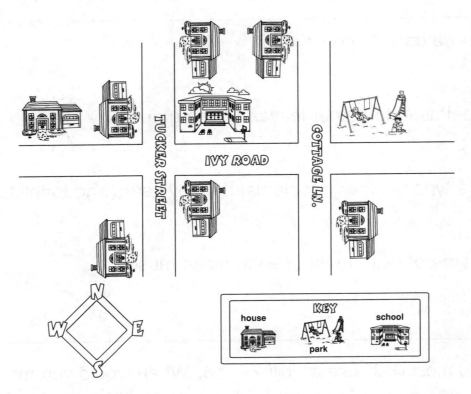

Use the map to help you answer the questions.

18. How many houses are on Tucker Street?
    Ⓐ four
    Ⓑ six
    Ⓒ ten
    Ⓓ twelve

19. Which direction would you travel from the school to the park?
    Ⓐ north
    Ⓑ south
    Ⓒ east
    Ⓓ west

20. How many total houses are on the map?
    Ⓐ 5
    Ⓑ 6
    Ⓒ 7
    Ⓓ 8

21. What road do you travel across to get from the park to the school?
    Ⓐ Cottage Lane
    Ⓑ Key Road
    Ⓒ Ivy Road
    Ⓓ Tucker Street

Sample Test

Directions: Fill in the circle next to the word or phrase that should go in the blank or substitute for the underlined words.

1. Kay _____ to Mexico on vacation.
   - Ⓐ go
   - Ⓑ went
   - Ⓒ going
   - Ⓓ goed

2. When did you _____?
   - Ⓐ leave
   - Ⓑ left
   - Ⓒ leaving
   - Ⓓ leaved

3. <u>Susan and I</u> like to watch movies.
   - Ⓐ Us
   - Ⓑ He
   - Ⓒ She
   - Ⓓ We

4. Please move the glass before <u>the glass</u> breaks.
   - Ⓐ they
   - Ⓑ it
   - Ⓒ them
   - Ⓓ she

Directions: Fill in the circle next to the part of the sentence that is <u>not</u> correct.

5.
   - Ⓐ She will be
   - Ⓑ eight years old
   - Ⓒ on she next birthday.

6.
   - Ⓐ Him and me
   - Ⓑ are best
   - Ⓒ friends.

7.
   - Ⓐ What time
   - Ⓑ do you want he
   - Ⓒ to arrive?

8.
   - Ⓐ The picture
   - Ⓑ hangs on the
   - Ⓒ wall along.

Directions: Fill in the circle next to the phrase that correctly completes each sentence.

9. The popcorn _____.
   - Ⓐ and ice cream
   - Ⓑ tasted
   - Ⓒ was salty
   - Ⓓ yummy

10. Mark and _____.
    - Ⓐ I
    - Ⓑ Oliver moved the truck
    - Ⓒ Scott go
    - Ⓓ Ray did before they

11. Brice _____.
    - Ⓐ gone
    - Ⓑ played soccer
    - Ⓒ was not in the
    - Ⓓ ate the soup with

Directions: Fill in the circle next to the complete sentence.

12.
   - Ⓐ Left the house later than expected.
   - Ⓑ Seven continents in the world.
   - Ⓒ We ride the bus to school.
   - Ⓓ To dance we go.

13.
   - Ⓐ Kyle likes to play outside.
   - Ⓑ Ride in the park.
   - Ⓒ After dinner we want.
   - Ⓓ Doesn't like the dentist.

14.
   - Ⓐ Before the sheep came.
   - Ⓑ Wore my warm gloves.
   - Ⓒ Watched a movie yesterday.
   - Ⓓ I like to eat olives.

Directions: Fill in the circle next to the phrase that is <u>not</u> part of a complete sentence.

15.
   - Ⓐ Becky finished
   - Ⓑ the book.
   - Ⓒ In one night.

16.
   - Ⓐ Loves to draw.
   - Ⓑ Dara is a
   - Ⓒ great illustrator.

17.
   - Ⓐ Brooke will go
   - Ⓑ to school tomorrow.
   - Ⓒ On vacation yesterday.

Directions: Fill in the circle next to the sentence that best completes each paragraph.

18. _____ I like to ride my bicycle in the neighborhood with friends. We usually ride to school and back.

Ⓐ Riding bicycles is a lot of fun!
Ⓑ Skateboarding is cool!
Ⓒ I live close to school.
Ⓓ I slept over at my grandma's house.

19. Playing hockey is great. _____ My favorite position to play is goalie.

Ⓐ I play baseball in the summer.
Ⓑ I ate chicken for dinner last night.
Ⓒ I have been playing since I was seven.
Ⓓ My dad likes to coach sports.

Directions: Read each sentence. Decide if it is a lead sentence in a paragraph or an ending sentence in a paragraph. Fill in the circle next to the correct answer.

20. As we drove along the highway, we saw many amazing sights.

Ⓐ lead
Ⓑ ending

21. Now you know, you must always brush your teeth before bed.

Ⓐ lead
Ⓑ ending

Becky is writing a letter to her mother about her snowboarding vacation.

22. What should Becky do before she writes the letter?

Ⓐ think about last summer
Ⓑ do her homework
Ⓒ think about her snowboarding vacation

23. What should her letter be about?

Ⓐ snowboarding
Ⓑ school
Ⓒ skiing

Name   Date

Directions: Fill in the circle next to the best title for each paragraph.

24. A paragraph about getting a new drum set.
    Ⓐ Playing in a Band
    Ⓑ Dancing
    Ⓒ My New Drums

25. A paragraph about training a puppy.
    Ⓐ Training Your New Puppy
    Ⓑ Training Your Cat
    Ⓒ Names for Your Puppy

26. A paragraph about putting on a puppet show.
    Ⓐ Puppets Are Fun
    Ⓑ Making a Puppet Show
    Ⓒ Different Kinds of Puppets

27. A paragraph about inventing a new kind of food.
    Ⓐ Easy-to-Make Recipes
    Ⓑ How to Make a New Recipe
    Ⓒ Using a Recipe to Make Dinner

| Name | Date |

Number Concepts

Directions: Read each question carefully. Fill in the circle next to the best answer for each question.

 Think about each question before you choose your answer.

Practice

1. Which number is less than 25?
   - Ⓐ 15
   - Ⓑ 52
   - Ⓒ 125
   - Ⓓ 30

2. Which number is less than 83?
   - Ⓐ 87
   - Ⓑ 46
   - Ⓒ 100
   - Ⓓ 90

3. Which number is more than 88?
   - Ⓐ 79
   - Ⓑ 29
   - Ⓒ 90
   - Ⓓ 62

4. Which number is more than 50?
   - Ⓐ 16
   - Ⓑ 49
   - Ⓒ 9
   - Ⓓ 72

5. Which number is between 43 and 59?
   - Ⓐ 17
   - Ⓑ 47
   - Ⓒ 84
   - Ⓓ 60

6. Which number is between 78 and 93?
   - Ⓐ 87
   - Ⓑ 97
   - Ⓒ 32
   - Ⓓ 69

Name _____ Date _____

7. What numbers are missing?
   20, 30, 40, ___, ___
   Ⓐ 45, 50
   Ⓑ 50, 60
   Ⓒ 41, 42
   Ⓓ 50, 40

8. What numbers are missing?
   34, 36, 38, ___, 42, ___
   Ⓐ 40, 44
   Ⓑ 40, 50
   Ⓒ 44, 46
   Ⓓ 39, 40

9. What numbers are missing?
   26, 27, ___, 29, ___
   Ⓐ 25, 23
   Ⓑ 30, 31
   Ⓒ 28, 30
   Ⓓ 25, 24

10. What numbers are missing?
   49, 48, 47, ___, ___
   Ⓐ 45, 44
   Ⓑ 46, 45
   Ⓒ 48, 49
   Ⓓ 50, 60

11. Match the number: four hundred sixty-two.
   Ⓐ 426
   Ⓑ 642
   Ⓒ 246
   Ⓓ 462

12. Match the number: two hundred thirty-nine.
   Ⓐ 200 + 30 + 9
   Ⓑ 2 + 300 + 90
   Ⓒ 20 + 3 + 900
   Ⓓ 2 + 30 + 900

13. Match the number: 876.
   Ⓐ eight thousand seventy-six
   Ⓑ eight hundred seventy-six
   Ⓒ eight hundred sixty-seven
   Ⓓ eighty-six

14. Match the number: 519.
   Ⓐ fifty-nine
   Ⓑ five hundred nine
   Ⓒ five hundred nineteen
   Ⓓ five thousand one hundred nine

15. Which group of numbers is in the correct counting order?

Ⓐ 73, 75, 74, 76
Ⓑ 73, 74, 75, 76
Ⓒ 73, 72, 74, 75
Ⓓ 73, 74, 76, 75

16. Which group of numbers is in the correct counting order?

Ⓐ 16, 17, 18, 19
Ⓑ 17, 16, 19, 18
Ⓒ 16, 17, 19, 18
Ⓓ 16, 18, 17, 19

17. What number is the difference between 9 and 19?

Ⓐ 9
Ⓑ 10
Ⓒ 11
Ⓓ 8

18. What number is the difference between 15 and 20?

Ⓐ 3
Ⓑ 5
Ⓒ 25
Ⓓ 35

19. Look at the group of stars.

Which group below has the same number?

20. Look at the group of shells.

Which group below has the same number?

Name _____   Date _____

Patterns

Directions: Read each question carefully. Fill in the circle next to the correct answer.

 If you are not sure of the correct answer, eliminate the answers you know are wrong; then make your best guess.

Practice

1. Which pattern is correct?
   - Ⓐ 60, 80, 20, 30
   - Ⓑ 60, 70, 80, 90
   - Ⓒ 65, 67, 87, 30
   - Ⓓ 60, 80, 70, 90

2. Which pattern is correct?
   - Ⓐ 3, 6, 9, 12
   - Ⓑ 3, 9, 6, 12
   - Ⓒ 3, 12, 9, 6
   - Ⓓ 6, 3, 9, 12

3. Which pattern is correct?
   - Ⓐ 45, 55, 60, 35
   - Ⓑ 45, 50, 30, 20
   - Ⓒ 45, 50, 55, 60
   - Ⓓ 8, 38, 28, 48

4. Which pattern is correct?
   - Ⓐ 78, 80, 82, 84
   - Ⓑ 78, 84, 82, 80
   - Ⓒ 78, 80, 84, 82
   - Ⓓ 80, 78, 84, 82

5. Complete the pattern.

   39, 42, 45, ___
   - Ⓐ 46
   - Ⓑ 48
   - Ⓒ 49
   - Ⓓ 47

6. Complete the pattern.

   44, 43, 42, ___
   - Ⓐ 43
   - Ⓑ 44
   - Ⓒ 40
   - Ⓓ 41

Test Prep Connection—Grade 2—RBP0857   www.summerbridgeactivities.com   ©RBP Books

7. What is another name for the following pattern?

  Ⓐ AB
  Ⓑ ABB
  Ⓒ ABC
  Ⓓ AAB

8. What is another name for the following pattern?

  Ⓐ AB
  Ⓑ ABB
  Ⓒ ABC
  Ⓓ AAB

9. Complete the pattern.

  Ⓐ ○
  Ⓑ ♡
  Ⓒ △
  Ⓓ □

10. Complete the pattern.

  Ⓐ 💡
  Ⓑ 🔨
  Ⓒ
  Ⓓ

Name   Date

Place Value

Directions: Read each question carefully. Fill in the circle next to the correct answer.

 Think about each answer before you make your final choice.

Practice

1. How many?
   - Ⓐ 10
   - Ⓑ 45
   - Ⓒ 64
   - Ⓓ 46

2.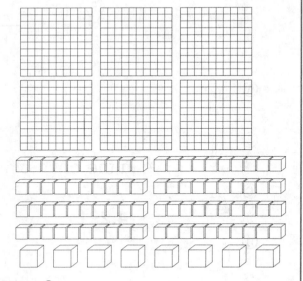
   How many?
   - Ⓐ 23
   - Ⓑ 88
   - Ⓒ 688
   - Ⓓ 868

3.

Hundreds	Tens	Ones
• • • • • • • • • •	• • • •	• •

   What number is represented?
   - Ⓐ 9,042
   - Ⓑ 942
   - Ⓒ 924
   - Ⓓ 9,024

4.

Hundreds	Tens	Ones
• • • • • •		• • •

   What number is represented?
   - Ⓐ 603
   - Ⓑ 6,003
   - Ⓒ 63
   - Ⓓ 630

GO ON

| Name | Date |

5. What digit is in the tens place?

4,710

- Ⓐ 4
- Ⓑ 7
- Ⓒ 1
- Ⓓ 0

6. What digit is in the ones place?

8,356

- Ⓐ 8
- Ⓑ 3
- Ⓒ 5
- Ⓓ 6

7. What digit is in the hundreds place?

9,327

- Ⓐ 9
- Ⓑ 3
- Ⓒ 2
- Ⓓ 7

8. What digit is in the tens place?

7,406

- Ⓐ 7
- Ⓑ 4
- Ⓒ 0
- Ⓓ 6

9. What digit is in the hundreds place?

1,735

- Ⓐ 1
- Ⓑ 7
- Ⓒ 3
- Ⓓ 5

10. What digit is in the ones place?

4,291

- Ⓐ 4
- Ⓑ 2
- Ⓒ 9
- Ⓓ 1

GO ON

Name _____   Date _____

11. Look at the number. What is the place value of the three?

738

Ⓐ ones
Ⓑ tens
Ⓒ hundreds

12. Look at the number. What is the place value of the five?

895

Ⓐ hundreds
Ⓑ tens
Ⓒ ones

13. Look at the number. What is the place value of the seven?

754

Ⓐ ones
Ⓑ hundreds
Ⓒ tens

14. Look at the number. What is the place value of the eight?

850

Ⓐ ones
Ⓑ tens
Ⓒ hundreds

15. Look at the number. What is the place value of the nine?

893

Ⓐ tens
Ⓑ ones
Ⓒ hundreds

16. Look at the number. What is the place value of the six?

126

Ⓐ hundreds
Ⓑ ones
Ⓒ tens

Test Prep Connection—Grade 2—RBP0857   www.summerbridgeactivities.com

17. Which number has 3 hundreds, 8 tens, and 7 ones?
 Ⓐ 873
 Ⓑ 387
 Ⓒ 783
 Ⓓ 837

18. Which number has 4 tens, 2 hundreds, and 9 ones?
 Ⓐ 429
 Ⓑ 294
 Ⓒ 249
 Ⓓ 942

19. Which number has 7 ones and 3 hundreds?
 Ⓐ 73
 Ⓑ 37
 Ⓒ 703
 Ⓓ 307

20. Which number has 5 ones, 8 hundreds, and 2 tens?
 Ⓐ 825
 Ⓑ 852
 Ⓒ 582
 Ⓓ 258

21. Which number has 1 ten and 9 hundreds?
 Ⓐ 19
 Ⓑ 91
 Ⓒ 901
 Ⓓ 910

22. Which number has 2 hundreds, 1 one, and 7 tens?
 Ⓐ 217
 Ⓑ 271
 Ⓒ 721
 Ⓓ 712

| Name | Date |

Properties

Directions: Read each question carefully. Fill in the circle next to the correct answer.

 Make sure you fill in the bubble next to the answer you think is correct. Look at each choice carefully before you select your final answer.

Practice

1. Look at each number sentence. Which is true?
   - Ⓐ 8 + 7 = 15
   - Ⓑ 8 ÷ 7 = 15
   - Ⓒ 8 x 7 = 15
   - Ⓓ 8 − 7 = 15

2. Look at each number sentence. Which is true?
   - Ⓐ 30 ÷ 20 = 10
   - Ⓑ 30 x 20 = 10
   - Ⓒ 30 − 20 = 10
   - Ⓓ 30 + 20 = 10

3. Look at each number sentence. Which is true?
   - Ⓐ 75 x 10 = 85
   - Ⓑ 75 ÷ 10 = 85
   - Ⓒ 75 − 10 = 85
   - Ⓓ 75 + 10 = 85

4. Which number statement means fifteen is greater than eleven?
   - Ⓐ 15 < 11
   - Ⓑ 15 > 11
   - Ⓒ 15 − 11
   - Ⓓ 11 > 15

5. Which number statement means four is less than twenty-four?
   - Ⓐ 4 < 24
   - Ⓑ 4 > 24
   - Ⓒ 24 < 4
   - Ⓓ 24 + 4

6. Which number statement means eight is equal to six plus two?
   - Ⓐ 8 > 6 + 2
   - Ⓑ 8 < 6 + 2
   - Ⓒ 8 = 6 + 2
   - Ⓓ 8 = 6 − 2

Name _____ Date _____

7. Which sign will make the number sentence correct?

19 ◯ 6 = 13

Ⓐ +
Ⓑ ÷
Ⓒ ×
Ⓓ −

8. Which sign will make the number sentence correct?

42 ◯ 20 = 62

Ⓐ ÷
Ⓑ −
Ⓒ +
Ⓓ ×

9. Which sign will make the number sentence correct?

89 ◯ 5 = 84

Ⓐ −
Ⓑ ÷
Ⓒ +
Ⓓ ×

10. What is the best estimate for the following number sentence?

47 + 32 = ◯

Ⓐ 50
Ⓑ 90
Ⓒ 80
Ⓓ 70

11. What is the best estimate for the following number sentence?

88 − 22 = ◯

Ⓐ 60
Ⓑ 80
Ⓒ 50
Ⓓ 70

12. What is the best estimate for the following number sentence?

17 + 39 = ◯

Ⓐ 60
Ⓑ 50
Ⓒ 70
Ⓓ 40

GO ON

13. Look at the table below. What is the "rule" that changes the "in" numbers to the "out" numbers?

In	Out
7	10
13	16
22	25
30	33

Ⓐ subtract 3
Ⓑ add 3
Ⓒ add 7
Ⓓ subtract 10

14. Look at the table below. What is the "rule" that changes the "in" numbers to the "out" numbers?

In	Out
2	4
4	8
8	16
16	32

Ⓐ add 2
Ⓑ add 4
Ⓒ double
Ⓓ half

15. Which group of number statements match the number below?

15

Ⓐ 8 + 6   and 20 − 5
Ⓑ 5 + 10 and 13 + 2
Ⓒ 9 + 4   and 18 − 3
Ⓓ 15 + 0 and 7 + 7

16. Which group of number statements match the number below?

28

Ⓐ 8 + 20 and 30 − 2
Ⓑ 20 − 2 and 22 + 8
Ⓒ 7 + 25 and 29 − 1
Ⓓ 20 + 8 and 18 − 10

| Name | Date |

Sample Test

Directions: Read each question carefully. Fill in the circle next to the correct answer.

1. What is the difference between 5 and 18?
   - Ⓐ 11
   - Ⓑ 15
   - Ⓒ 13
   - Ⓓ 10

2. What number is missing on the number line?

   0, 2, 4, 8, 10, 12

   - Ⓐ 5
   - Ⓑ 6
   - Ⓒ 7
   - Ⓓ 1

3. Which child is third in line?

   Ⓐ Ⓑ Ⓒ Ⓓ

4. What number matches eight hundred sixty-four?
   - Ⓐ 846
   - Ⓑ 648
   - Ⓒ 814
   - Ⓓ 864

5. What number matches four hundred two?
   - Ⓐ 42
   - Ⓑ 420
   - Ⓒ 402
   - Ⓓ 4,002

6. What number is missing?
   fifteen, sixteen, _____, eighteen
   - Ⓐ fourteen
   - Ⓑ seventeen
   - Ⓒ twelve
   - Ⓓ twenty

7. What number is missing?
   twenty, _____, thirty, thirty-five
   - Ⓐ twenty-one
   - Ⓑ twenty-five
   - Ⓒ twenty-nine
   - Ⓓ nineteen

GO ON

8. What word matches the number in the middle?

   8, 9, 10, 11, 12

   Ⓐ eight
   Ⓑ nine
   Ⓒ ten
   Ⓓ eleven

9. What word matches the number in the middle?

   88, 89, 90, 91, 92, 93, 94

   Ⓐ ninety-one
   Ⓑ ninety-two
   Ⓒ ninety-three
   Ⓓ ninety

10. What comes next?

    Ⓐ
    Ⓑ
    Ⓒ
    Ⓓ

11. What is another name for the following pattern?

    Ⓐ AB
    Ⓑ ABC
    Ⓒ ABB
    Ⓓ AAB

12. Look at the numbers below. Which number does not belong?

    6, 9, 12, 15, 16, 18

    Ⓐ 18
    Ⓑ 16
    Ⓒ 12
    Ⓓ 9

13. Look at the number below. Which number is in the tens place?

    850

    Ⓐ 8
    Ⓑ 5
    Ⓒ 0

GO ON

14. Look at the number below. What is the place value of the four?

439

Ⓐ hundreds
Ⓑ tens
Ⓒ ones

15. What number has six tens and three ones?

Ⓐ 36
Ⓑ 360
Ⓒ 463

16. What number has five ones and seven hundreds?

Ⓐ 795 Ⓑ 57
Ⓒ 507 Ⓓ 753

17. Look at the place value chart below. Which number matches the number represented?

Hundreds	Tens	Ones
/ / /	/ / / / / / / /	/ /

Ⓐ 832 Ⓑ 382
Ⓒ 238 Ⓓ 328

18. What is 32 rounded to the nearest ten?

Ⓐ 20
Ⓑ 35
Ⓒ 30
Ⓓ 40

19. Which number statement means sixteen is greater than twelve?

Ⓐ 16 > 12
Ⓑ 16 + 12
Ⓒ 16 < 12
Ⓓ 16 = 12

20. Which sign will make the number sentence correct?

72 ○ 12 = 60

Ⓐ −
Ⓑ +
Ⓒ ×
Ⓓ ÷

| Name | Date |

Addition

Directions: Solve each addition problem. Fill in the circle next to the correct answer.

Examples:

A. 8 + 3 =
- Ⓐ 10
- ● 11
- Ⓒ 14
- Ⓓ 12

B. 7 + 5 =
- ● 12
- Ⓒ 11
- Ⓑ 13
- Ⓓ 15

Hint: Work out each problem even if you think you know the answer.

Practice

1. 45
   + 12

   - Ⓐ 56
   - Ⓑ 57
   - Ⓒ 58
   - Ⓓ 67

2. 39 + 16 =
   - Ⓐ 55
   - Ⓑ 56
   - Ⓒ 54
   - Ⓓ 65

3. 412
   + 68

   - Ⓐ 500
   - Ⓑ 420
   - Ⓒ 479
   - Ⓓ 480

4. 89 + 20 =
   - Ⓐ 99
   - Ⓑ 119
   - Ⓒ 109
   - Ⓓ 129

5. $37
   + $27

   - Ⓐ $10
   - Ⓑ $64
   - Ⓒ $87
   - Ⓓ $77

6. 8 + 8 + 8 =
   - Ⓐ 24
   - Ⓑ 16
   - Ⓒ 23
   - Ⓓ 18

GO ON →

7.
```
   8
   4
 + 9
```
Ⓐ 20   Ⓑ 21
Ⓒ 22   Ⓓ 23

8. 704 + 145 =
Ⓐ 809   Ⓑ 829
Ⓒ 839   Ⓓ 849

9. 81 + 68 =
Ⓐ 150
Ⓑ 139
Ⓒ 149
Ⓓ 140

10.
```
   30
   50
 + 10
```
Ⓐ 80   Ⓑ 90
Ⓒ 100 Ⓓ 70

11. 7 + 40 + 200 =
Ⓐ 247   Ⓑ 742
Ⓒ 427   Ⓓ 274

12.
```
   93
 + 39
```
Ⓐ 122   Ⓑ 142
Ⓒ 133   Ⓓ 132

13. 45 + ___ = 50
Ⓐ 15   Ⓑ 20
Ⓒ 5   Ⓓ 10

14. ___ + 8 = 40
Ⓐ 33   Ⓑ 32
Ⓒ 30   Ⓓ 22

15. 35 + 8 =
- Ⓐ 44
- Ⓑ 45
- Ⓒ 42
- Ⓓ 43

16. $8 + $58 =
- Ⓐ $66
- Ⓑ $67
- Ⓒ $68
- Ⓓ $65

17.
```
    9
    7
　+ 3
```
- Ⓐ 18
- Ⓑ 19
- Ⓒ 20
- Ⓓ 21

18.
```
   29
   56
 + 32
```
- Ⓐ 115
- Ⓑ 117
- Ⓒ 119
- Ⓓ 121

19. 22 + ___ = 29
- Ⓐ 6
- Ⓑ 7
- Ⓒ 8
- Ⓓ 9

20. 31 + 46 + 68 =
- Ⓐ 144
- Ⓑ 145
- Ⓒ 77
- Ⓓ 146

21.
```
    8
 + 26
```
- Ⓐ 30
- Ⓑ 36
- Ⓒ 34
- Ⓓ 35

22.
```
   17
 + 53
```
- Ⓐ 60
- Ⓑ 50
- Ⓒ 80
- Ⓓ 70

STOP

Name   Date

Subtraction

Directions: Solve each subtraction problem. Fill in the circle next to the correct answer.

Examples:

A. 24 − 4 =
- Ⓐ 4
- ● 20
- Ⓒ 19
- Ⓓ 21

B. 9 − 5 =
- Ⓐ 5
- ● 4
- Ⓑ 3
- Ⓓ 6

 Work out each problem even if you think you know the answer.

Practice

1. 72 − 42 =
   - Ⓐ 32
   - Ⓑ 30
   - Ⓒ 40
   - Ⓓ 34

2.   27
    − 16
   - Ⓐ 11
   - Ⓑ 10
   - Ⓒ 21
   - Ⓓ 12

3.   70
    − 50
   - Ⓐ 12
   - Ⓑ 2
   - Ⓒ 10
   - Ⓓ 20

4. 85 − 79 =
   - Ⓐ 16
   - Ⓑ 26
   - Ⓒ 6
   - Ⓓ 61

5. 989 − 6 =
   - Ⓐ 929
   - Ⓑ 983
   - Ⓒ 389
   - Ⓓ 982

6. $71
    − $32
   - Ⓐ $40
   - Ⓑ $38
   - Ⓒ $39
   - Ⓓ $37

GO ON

7. 348
   − 19

   Ⓐ 329   Ⓑ 330
   Ⓒ 327   Ⓓ 328

8. 75 − 25 =
   Ⓐ 50   Ⓑ 40
   Ⓒ 30   Ⓓ 25

9. 821
   − 511

   Ⓐ 311   Ⓑ 320
   Ⓒ 210   Ⓓ 310

10. 64 − 22 =
    Ⓐ 40   Ⓑ 42
    Ⓒ 44   Ⓓ 48

11. 258 − 158 =
    Ⓐ 101   Ⓑ 100
    Ⓒ 99   Ⓓ 90

12. $83
    − $72

    Ⓐ $15   Ⓑ $12
    Ⓒ $11   Ⓓ $10

13. 86 − 13 =
    Ⓐ 72   Ⓑ 70
    Ⓒ 74   Ⓓ 73

14. 265 − 8 =
    Ⓐ 257   Ⓑ 253
    Ⓒ 258   Ⓓ 256

GO ON

15. 478
    −470

Ⓐ 470   Ⓑ 8
Ⓒ 78   Ⓓ 80

16. 764
    −715

Ⓐ 50   Ⓑ 51
Ⓒ 49   Ⓓ 39

17. 21 − 7 =

Ⓐ 13   Ⓑ 14
Ⓒ 12   Ⓓ 11

18. 59 − 4 =

Ⓐ 19   Ⓑ 54
Ⓒ 63   Ⓓ 55

19. 930 − 45 =

Ⓐ 885   Ⓑ 895
Ⓒ 905   Ⓓ 875

20. 361
    − 21

Ⓐ 330   Ⓑ 340
Ⓒ 320   Ⓓ 310

21. 63 − 22 =

Ⓐ 40   Ⓑ 41
Ⓒ 42   Ⓓ 43

22. 375
    − 86

Ⓐ 290
Ⓑ 189
Ⓒ 289
Ⓓ 389

STOP

| Name | Date |

Addition and Subtraction

Directions: Look at each question carefully. Fill in the circle next to the correct answer.

Examples:

A. 8 + 5 =
Ⓐ 12   ● 13
Ⓒ 14   Ⓓ 15

B. 17 − 6 =
Ⓐ 9   Ⓑ 10
● 11   Ⓓ 12

 Look carefully at the sign in each problem. Should you add or subtract?

Practice

1. 90 + 90 =
   Ⓐ 190   Ⓑ 180
   Ⓒ 109   Ⓓ 108

2.   732
   − 182

   Ⓐ 500   Ⓑ 450
   Ⓒ 650   Ⓓ 550

3.   89
   + 8

   Ⓐ 99   Ⓑ 97
   Ⓒ 98   Ⓓ 96

4. 51 − 46 =
   Ⓐ 15   Ⓑ 4
   Ⓒ 5   Ⓓ 11

5. 267 − 15 =
   Ⓐ 252   Ⓑ 52
   Ⓒ 152   Ⓓ 262

6. 743 + 91 =
   Ⓐ 734   Ⓑ 943
   Ⓒ 834   Ⓓ 883

GO ON

Name _____   Date _____

7. 500
   −450

   Ⓐ 150   Ⓑ 50
   Ⓒ 45   Ⓓ 145

8. 93 + 54 =
   Ⓐ 144   Ⓑ 146
   Ⓒ 147   Ⓓ 141

9. 402 − 102 =
   Ⓐ 300   Ⓑ 200
   Ⓒ 302   Ⓓ 102

10. 825
    + 70

   Ⓐ 905   Ⓑ 875
   Ⓒ 885   Ⓓ 895

11. 733
   − 79

   Ⓐ 656   Ⓑ 657
   Ⓒ 654   Ⓓ 655

12. 44 − 35 =
   Ⓐ 11   Ⓑ 9
   Ⓒ 12   Ⓓ 8

13. 226
   −139

   Ⓐ 88   Ⓑ 87
   Ⓒ 86   Ⓓ 83

14. 63 + 98 =
   Ⓐ 162   Ⓑ 161
   Ⓒ 164   Ⓓ 154

15. 741
    −472

Ⓐ 271   Ⓑ 269
Ⓒ 279   Ⓓ 261

16. 25 + 27 =

Ⓐ 53   Ⓑ 54
Ⓒ 52   Ⓓ 51

17.   19
     4
   +7

Ⓐ 29   Ⓑ 28
Ⓒ 30   Ⓓ 31

18. 6 + 4 + 2 =

Ⓐ 11   Ⓑ 10
Ⓒ 9   Ⓓ 12

19. 86 − 12 =

Ⓐ 72   Ⓑ 73
Ⓒ 74   Ⓓ 75

20. $75
   −$12

Ⓐ $67   Ⓑ $87
Ⓒ $63   Ⓓ $97

21. 81 − 11 =

Ⓐ 80   Ⓑ 70
Ⓒ 60   Ⓓ 71

22. 35 + 35 + 35 =

Ⓐ 75   Ⓑ 100
Ⓒ 110   Ⓓ 105

| Name | Date |

Multiplication

Directions: Look at each question carefully. Fill in the circle next to the correct answer.

Examples:

A. 2 × 3 =
  Ⓐ 5   ● 6
  Ⓒ 9   Ⓓ 4

B. 4 × 1 =
  Ⓐ 5   Ⓑ 3
  Ⓒ 8   ● 4

 Remember, you are multiplying. Use the space provided to work out your answer.

Practice

1.

   Which number sentence matches the array?
   Ⓐ 4 × 2 = 8   Ⓑ 4 × 4 = 16
   Ⓒ 4 × 5 = 20   Ⓓ 4 × 3 = 12

2.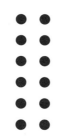

   Which number sentence matches the array?
   Ⓐ 6 × 6 = 36   Ⓑ 6 × 1 = 6
   Ⓒ 6 × 2 = 12   Ⓓ 6 × 4 = 24

3.

   Which number sentence matches the array?
   Ⓐ 2 × 5 = 10   Ⓑ 2 × 2 = 4
   Ⓒ 5 + 2 = 7   Ⓓ 5 × 10 = 50

4.

   Which number sentence matches the array?
   Ⓐ 5 + 5 = 10   Ⓑ 5 × 5 = 25
   Ⓒ 5 × 2 = 10   Ⓓ 5 × 4 = 20

Name _____   Date _____

5.   3
     x 3
     ───
   Ⓐ 9   Ⓑ 6
   Ⓒ 33   Ⓓ 1

6. 9 x 2 =
   Ⓐ 11   Ⓑ 92
   Ⓒ 7   Ⓓ 18

7. 5 x 4 =
   Ⓐ 25   Ⓑ 20
   Ⓒ 9   Ⓓ 1

8.   10
     x 4
     ───
   Ⓐ 14   Ⓑ 41
   Ⓒ 400   Ⓓ 40

9.   3
     x 5
     ───
   Ⓐ 2   Ⓑ 15
   Ⓒ 8   Ⓓ 20

10. 9 x 0 =
   Ⓐ 9   Ⓑ 90
   Ⓒ 99   Ⓓ 0

11.   6
     x 3
     ───
   Ⓐ 3   Ⓑ 9
   Ⓒ 19   Ⓓ 18

12. 7 x 5 =
   Ⓐ 30   Ⓑ 35
   Ⓒ 12   Ⓓ 36

| Name | Date |

Division

Directions: Look at each question carefully. Fill in the circle next to the correct answer.

Examples:

A. 12 ÷ 6 =
- Ⓐ 6
- ● 2
- Ⓒ 3
- Ⓓ 9

B. 3)9
- Ⓐ 6
- Ⓑ 12
- ● 3
- Ⓓ 2

Be sure you are dividing. If you are unsure of an answer, skip the problem and come back to it at the end.

Practice

1. 20 ÷ 2 =
   - Ⓐ 18
   - Ⓑ 22
   - Ⓒ 40
   - Ⓓ 10

2. 3)24
   - Ⓐ 8
   - Ⓑ 18
   - Ⓒ 21
   - Ⓓ 27

3. 15 ÷ 3 =
   - Ⓐ 12
   - Ⓑ 5
   - Ⓒ 18
   - Ⓓ 28

4. 1)7
   - Ⓐ 8
   - Ⓑ 6
   - Ⓒ 7
   - Ⓓ 17

5. 4)16
   - Ⓐ 4
   - Ⓑ 20
   - Ⓒ 12
   - Ⓓ 24

6. 18 ÷ 9 =
   - Ⓐ 27
   - Ⓑ 9
   - Ⓒ 3
   - Ⓓ 2

| Name | Date |

Sample Test

Directions: Read each question carefully. Fill in the circle next to the correct answer.

1.   96
  + 15

   Ⓐ 110   Ⓑ 111
   Ⓒ 112   Ⓓ 1,011

2. 30 + ___ = 45
   Ⓐ 5
   Ⓑ 10
   Ⓒ 15
   Ⓓ 25

3. 18 − 9 =
   Ⓐ 27
   Ⓑ 8
   Ⓒ 28
   Ⓓ 9

4.   45
  − 7

   Ⓐ 32   Ⓑ 39
   Ⓒ 38   Ⓓ 42

5. 3 + 8 + 5 =
   Ⓐ 16
   Ⓑ 15
   Ⓒ 18
   Ⓓ 26

6.   834
  − 248

   Ⓐ 586   Ⓑ 587
   Ⓒ 686   Ⓓ 684

7. 31 + 56 =
   Ⓐ 85
   Ⓑ 87
   Ⓒ 88
   Ⓓ 25

8. 94 − 55 =
   Ⓐ 38
   Ⓑ 37
   Ⓒ 48
   Ⓓ 39

GO ON

Name _____   Date _____

9. 200 − 157 =
  Ⓐ 143
  Ⓑ 44
  Ⓒ 47
  Ⓓ 43

10. 76 + 28 =
  Ⓐ 114
  Ⓑ 104
  Ⓒ 124
  Ⓓ 94

11. 61
   + 38

  Ⓐ 99
  Ⓑ 89
  Ⓒ 79
  Ⓓ 109

12. 806 − 205 =
  Ⓐ 611
  Ⓑ 621
  Ⓒ 651
  Ⓓ 601

13. 53
   − 36

  Ⓐ 17
  Ⓑ 19
  Ⓒ 29
  Ⓓ 27

14. 45 − 14 =
  Ⓐ 41
  Ⓑ 31
  Ⓒ 21
  Ⓓ 11

15. 492
   + 128

  Ⓐ 630
  Ⓑ 610
  Ⓒ 620
  Ⓓ 626

16. 19 − ___ = 7
  Ⓐ 12
  Ⓑ 26
  Ⓒ 16
  Ⓓ 11

Name _____ **Date** _____

17. 8
   5
  +7

Ⓐ 22 Ⓑ 20
Ⓒ 21 Ⓓ 19

18. ___ + 11 = 100

Ⓐ 91
Ⓑ 79
Ⓒ 89
Ⓓ 92

19. 95 − ___ = 45

Ⓐ 50
Ⓑ 55
Ⓒ 45
Ⓓ 35

20.   83
   −14

Ⓐ 67 Ⓑ 68
Ⓒ 69 Ⓓ 71

21. 8 x ___ = 16

Ⓐ 3
Ⓑ 4
Ⓒ 2
Ⓓ 1

22. 7 x 3 =

Ⓐ 18
Ⓑ 21
Ⓒ 24
Ⓓ 19

23. 3 x 4 =

Ⓐ 16
Ⓑ 20
Ⓒ 9
Ⓓ 12

24. 7 x 1 =

Ⓐ 8
Ⓑ 14
Ⓒ 7
Ⓓ 1

Name _____ Date _____

25. 8 × ___ = 40
- Ⓐ 6
- Ⓑ 5
- Ⓒ 4
- Ⓓ 20

26. 9 × 2 =
- Ⓐ 18
- Ⓑ 11
- Ⓒ 24
- Ⓓ 16

27. 7 × 5 =
- Ⓐ 25
- Ⓑ 30
- Ⓒ 35
- Ⓓ 40

28. 8 × 4 =
- Ⓐ 24
- Ⓑ 36
- Ⓒ 35
- Ⓓ 32

29. 5) 25
- Ⓐ 50
- Ⓑ 4
- Ⓒ 5
- Ⓓ 6

30. 14 ÷ 7 =
- Ⓐ 2
- Ⓑ 7
- Ⓒ 21
- Ⓓ 8

31. 60 ÷ 6 =
- Ⓐ 6
- Ⓑ 11
- Ⓒ 66
- Ⓓ 10

32. 4) 24
- Ⓐ 6
- Ⓑ 16
- Ⓒ 28
- Ⓓ 20

STOP

Name _____ Date _____

Time

Directions: Fill in the circle next to the correct answer.

Examples: A. What time does the clock show?
- ● 7:30
- Ⓑ 6:35
- Ⓒ 7:35
- Ⓓ 8:30

B. Match the times.

Ⓐ ●

Ⓒ Ⓓ

Hint: Remember, the long hand shows the minute, and the short hand shows the hour.

Practice

1. Which clock shows half past four?

   Ⓐ   Ⓑ

   Ⓒ   Ⓓ

3. Which clock shows a quarter past one?

   Ⓐ   Ⓑ

   Ⓒ   Ⓓ

2. Which clock shows a quarter to nine?

   Ⓐ   Ⓑ

   Ⓒ   Ⓓ

4. Which clock shows 3:25?

   Ⓐ   Ⓑ

   Ⓒ   Ⓓ

GO ON

| Name | Date |

5. Which clock shows 12:50?

Ⓐ   Ⓑ

Ⓒ   Ⓓ

6. Which clock shows 5:15?

Ⓐ   Ⓑ

Ⓒ   Ⓓ

7. Which clock shows 9:15?

Ⓐ   Ⓑ

Ⓒ   Ⓓ

8. Jimmy leaves for school in the morning. What time does Jimmy probably leave for school?

Ⓐ 8:00 p.m.
Ⓑ 12:00 p.m.
Ⓒ 8:00 a.m.
Ⓓ 3:00 a.m.

9. The Miller family eats dinner before bedtime. What time does the Miller family probably eat dinner?

Ⓐ 3:00 p.m.
Ⓑ 6:30 p.m.
Ⓒ 11:00 p.m.
Ⓓ 2:30 a.m.

10. Jill takes the dog for a walk right after lunch. What time does Jill probably take the dog for a walk?

Ⓐ 4:30 p.m.
Ⓑ 1:00 a.m.
Ⓒ 1:00 p.m.
Ⓓ 9:00 a.m.

GO ON

Name _____   Date _____

11. Match the times.
  Ⓐ 9:20
  Ⓑ 8:20
  Ⓒ 4:45
  Ⓓ 5:45

12. Match the times.
  Ⓐ 1:10
  Ⓑ 2:05
  Ⓒ 1:05
  Ⓓ 2:10

13. Match the times.

14. Match the times.

15. Brenda started reading a book at 7:00. It took her fifteen minutes to finish the book. What time did Brenda finish the book?

Ⓐ   Ⓑ

Ⓒ   Ⓓ

16. It took Milton ten minutes to walk to school. He arrived at school at 8:00. What time did Milton leave?

Ⓐ   Ⓑ

Ⓒ   Ⓓ

17. Henry ran two miles in twenty-five minutes. He finished at 1:30. What time did Henry begin running?

Ⓐ   Ⓑ

Ⓒ   Ⓓ

GO ON

February

Sunday	Monday	Tuesday	Wednesday	Thursday	Friday	Saturday
		1	2	3	4	5
6	7	8 Kevin's birthday	9	10	11	12
13	14 Valentine's Day	15	16	17	18	19
20	21	22	23	24	25	26
27	28	29				

Directions: Use the calendar to answer the following questions.

18. What day of the week is the first day of February?

Ⓐ Monday
Ⓑ Tuesday
Ⓒ Wednesday
Ⓓ Thursday

19. What day of the week is Valentine's Day?

Ⓐ Sunday
Ⓑ Monday
Ⓒ Tuesday
Ⓓ Wednesday

20. What day of the week is February 26?

Ⓐ Monday
Ⓑ Wednesday
Ⓒ Thursday
Ⓓ Saturday

21. When is Kevin's birthday?

Ⓐ February 18
Ⓑ February 8
Ⓒ February 11
Ⓓ February 25

22. How many days after Kevin's birthday is Valentine's Day?

Ⓐ 5
Ⓑ 6
Ⓒ 7
Ⓓ 9

Name _____ Date _____

Money

Directions: Fill in the circle next to the correct answer.

Examples:

A. How much money?
- ● 25¢
- Ⓑ 30¢
- Ⓒ 15¢
- Ⓓ 35¢

B. How much money?
- Ⓐ 21¢
- Ⓑ 30¢
- Ⓒ 55¢
- ● 51¢

Remember the value of each coin. Count the coins that are worth the most first.

Practice

1. How much money?
   - Ⓐ 30¢
   - Ⓑ 25¢
   - Ⓒ 16¢
   - Ⓓ 3¢

2. How much money?
   - Ⓐ 75¢
   - Ⓑ 27¢
   - Ⓒ 37¢
   - Ⓓ 17¢

3. How much money?
   - Ⓐ 28¢
   - Ⓑ 23¢
   - Ⓒ 33¢
   - Ⓓ 37¢

4. How much money?
   - Ⓐ 51¢
   - Ⓑ 33¢
   - Ⓒ 42¢
   - Ⓓ 47¢

5. How much money?
   - Ⓐ 35¢
   - Ⓑ 37¢
   - Ⓒ 19¢
   - Ⓓ 29¢

6. How much money?
   - Ⓐ 15¢
   - Ⓑ 26¢
   - Ⓒ 42¢
   - Ⓓ 27¢

   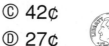

Test Prep Connection—Grade 2—RBP0857

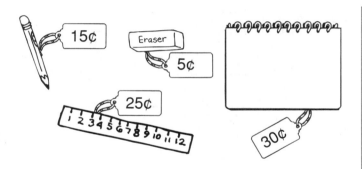
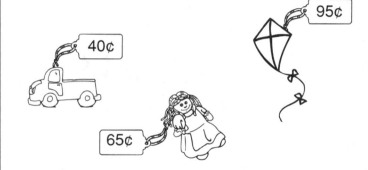

7. Polly has 50¢. Does she have enough money to buy one pencil and two rulers?

    Ⓐ yes   Ⓑ no

8. Taylor has $1. He buys two erasers and one notebook. What is his change?

    Ⓐ 70¢
    Ⓑ 40¢
    Ⓒ 60¢
    Ⓓ 65¢

9. William has three quarters. He buys two notebooks. What is his change?

    Ⓐ 15¢
    Ⓑ 25¢
    Ⓒ 5¢
    Ⓓ 20¢

10. Malloree has two quarters and one dime. Does she have enough money to buy a doll?

    Ⓐ yes   Ⓑ no

11. Colin has 75¢. He buys a toy truck. What is his change?

    Ⓐ 45¢
    Ⓑ 25¢
    Ⓒ 40¢
    Ⓓ 35¢

12. Simon has $1. He buys a kite. What is his change?

    Ⓐ 10¢
    Ⓑ 15¢
    Ⓒ 5¢
    Ⓓ 25¢

Name _____ Date _____

13.

How much money?

Ⓐ $32.45
Ⓑ $50.54
Ⓒ $32.54
Ⓓ $23.54

14.

How much money?

Ⓐ $65.95
Ⓑ $56.95
Ⓒ $11.85
Ⓓ $56.85

15.

How much money?

Ⓐ $28.52
Ⓑ $10.52
Ⓒ $82.52
Ⓓ $28.07

16.

How much money?

Ⓐ $12.30
Ⓑ $30.12
Ⓒ $39.60
Ⓓ $39.30

Name   Date

Estimation

Directions: Fill in the circle next to the best estimated answer.

Examples: **A.** Choose the best estimate.   **B.** Choose the best estimate.

$$36 + 12 =$$

Ⓐ 40   ● 50
© 60   Ⓓ 70

$$71 + 16 =$$

Ⓐ 70   Ⓑ 80
● 90   Ⓓ 100

 Estimating means you round the number to the closest ten or hundred.

Practice

1. 49 + 12 =
   Ⓐ 30
   Ⓑ 40
   © 50
   Ⓓ 60

2. 32 + 19 =
   Ⓐ 40
   Ⓑ 50
   © 60
   Ⓓ 70

3. 612 + 209 =
   Ⓐ 700
   Ⓑ 800
   © 900
   Ⓓ 750

4.   96
    + 22

   Ⓐ 100   Ⓑ 110
   © 120   Ⓓ 130

5.   56
    + 11

   Ⓐ 55   Ⓑ 60
   © 70   Ⓓ 75

6. 81 + 52 =
   Ⓐ 130
   Ⓑ 125
   © 120
   Ⓓ 140

7. 308 + 278 =
   Ⓐ 550
   Ⓑ 500
   Ⓒ 650
   Ⓓ 600

8. 7 + 12 + 22 =
   Ⓐ 30
   Ⓑ 40
   Ⓒ 50
   Ⓓ 35

9. 3 + 29 =
   Ⓐ 25
   Ⓑ 35
   Ⓒ 40
   Ⓓ 30

10. 45 + 66 =
    Ⓐ 120
    Ⓑ 100
    Ⓒ 130
    Ⓓ 125

11. 81
    + 37

    Ⓐ 100
    Ⓑ 110
    Ⓒ 120
    Ⓓ 130

12. 799
    + 101

    Ⓐ 800
    Ⓑ 850
    Ⓒ 950
    Ⓓ 900

13. 54 + 30 =
    Ⓐ 70
    Ⓑ 90
    Ⓒ 80
    Ⓓ 75

14. 21
    + 48

    Ⓐ 70
    Ⓑ 65
    Ⓒ 60
    Ⓓ 75

15. 72 + 148 =

Ⓐ 200
Ⓑ 210
Ⓒ 220
Ⓓ 230

16. 46
 + 27

Ⓐ 80
Ⓑ 85
Ⓒ 90
Ⓓ 65

17. 93 + 11 =

Ⓐ 110
Ⓑ 100
Ⓒ 105
Ⓓ 95

18. 71 + 51 =

Ⓐ 125
Ⓑ 105
Ⓒ 110
Ⓓ 120

19. 33
 + 88

Ⓐ 120
Ⓑ 135
Ⓒ 150
Ⓓ 160

20. 409 + 277 =

Ⓐ 600
Ⓑ 800
Ⓒ 650
Ⓓ 700

21. 26 + 19 =

Ⓐ 50
Ⓑ 30
Ⓒ 40
Ⓓ 60

22. 74
 + 8

Ⓐ 85
Ⓑ 80
Ⓒ 95
Ⓓ 90

| Name | Date |

Fractions

Directions: Fill in the circle next to the correct answer.

Examples: A. What fraction of the square is shaded?
- ● $\frac{1}{2}$
- Ⓑ $\frac{1}{3}$
- Ⓒ $\frac{1}{4}$
- Ⓓ $\frac{2}{3}$

B. What fraction tells how many are hearts?
- Ⓐ $\frac{1}{2}$
- Ⓑ $\frac{1}{4}$
- Ⓒ $\frac{1}{3}$
- ● $\frac{2}{3}$

 Fractions are never whole numbers.

Practice

1. What fraction of the triangle is <u>not</u> shaded?
   - Ⓐ $\frac{2}{3}$
   - Ⓑ $\frac{1}{4}$
   - Ⓒ $\frac{1}{2}$
   - Ⓓ $\frac{4}{5}$

3. What fraction of the rectangle is shaded?
   - Ⓐ $\frac{2}{3}$
   - Ⓑ $\frac{1}{4}$
   - Ⓒ $\frac{1}{2}$
   - Ⓓ $\frac{4}{5}$

2. What fraction of the circle is shaded?
   - Ⓐ $\frac{5}{8}$
   - Ⓑ $\frac{4}{8}$
   - Ⓒ $\frac{6}{8}$
   - Ⓓ $\frac{7}{8}$

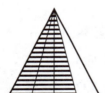

4. What fraction tells how many children are girls?

   - Ⓐ $\frac{2}{6}$
   - Ⓑ $\frac{2}{8}$
   - Ⓒ $\frac{1}{3}$
   - Ⓓ $\frac{4}{8}$

5. What fraction of the hexagon is not shaded?

Ⓐ $\frac{1}{2}$
Ⓑ $\frac{2}{6}$
Ⓒ $\frac{4}{6}$
Ⓓ $\frac{1}{6}$

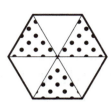

6. What fraction of the animals are frogs?

Ⓐ $\frac{1}{5}$
Ⓑ $\frac{2}{5}$
Ⓒ $\frac{3}{5}$
Ⓓ $\frac{4}{5}$

7. What fraction of the circle is shaded?

Ⓐ $\frac{1}{2}$
Ⓑ $\frac{2}{3}$
Ⓒ $\frac{1}{3}$
Ⓓ $\frac{3}{3}$

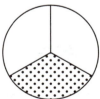

8. What fraction of the illustrations are umbrellas?

Ⓐ $\frac{2}{4}$
Ⓑ $\frac{2}{3}$
Ⓒ $\frac{3}{4}$
Ⓓ $\frac{2}{6}$

9. What fraction of the rectangle is shaded?

Ⓐ $\frac{1}{2}$
Ⓑ $\frac{1}{3}$
Ⓒ $\frac{1}{4}$
Ⓓ $\frac{2}{4}$

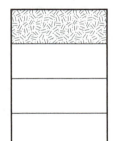

10. Which one shows 5 of 9 equal parts shaded?

Ⓐ 　　Ⓑ

Ⓒ 　　Ⓓ

Name _____ Date _____

Measurement

Directions: Fill in the circle next to the correct answer.

Examples: **A.** Use the ruler to measure the pencil. How long is the pencil?
- Ⓐ 5 centimeters
- ● 5 inches
- Ⓒ $5\frac{1}{2}$ inches
- Ⓓ 6 inches

B. Which thermometer shows 80° F?

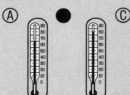
Ⓐ ● Ⓒ Ⓓ

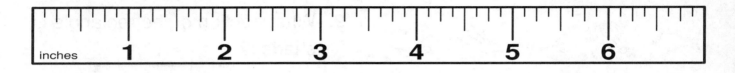

Hint:  Remember to check the instrument you are using to measure. Are you measuring by inches or centimeters?

Practice

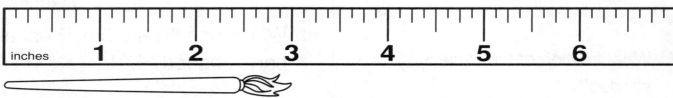

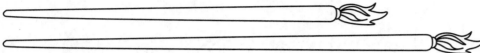

1. What is the measurement of the shortest paintbrush?
   - Ⓐ 3 inches
   - Ⓑ 4 inches
   - Ⓒ 3 centimeters
   - Ⓓ 5 centimeters

2. What is the measurement of the longest paintbrush?
   - Ⓐ 4 inches
   - Ⓑ 5 centimeters
   - Ⓒ 4 centimeters
   - Ⓓ 5 inches

Name Date

3. What temperature does the thermometer show?

Ⓐ 33°F Ⓑ 34°F
Ⓒ 32°F Ⓓ 31°F

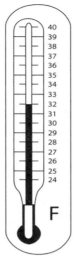

4. What temperature does the thermometer show?

Ⓐ 76°F Ⓑ 77°F
Ⓒ 78°F Ⓓ 75°F

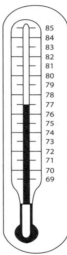

5. Which will hold the most?

Ⓐ   Ⓑ
Ⓒ   Ⓓ

6. Which will hold the least?

Ⓐ   Ⓑ
Ⓒ   Ⓓ

7. Which picture shows 1 cup?

Ⓐ   Ⓑ
Ⓒ   Ⓓ

8. Which picture shows 1 pint?

Ⓐ   Ⓑ
Ⓒ   Ⓓ

| Name | Date |

Geometry

Directions: Fill in the circle next to the correct answer.

Examples: A. Which figure below has symmetry?   B. Which of the following is a cone?

Hint: Use key words and the pictures to help you find the answer to each problem.

Practice

1. Which of the following is a pyramid?

2. Which of the following is a cylinder?

3. What is the shape below?

   Ⓐ sphere
   Ⓑ cube
   Ⓒ cone
   Ⓓ rectangular prism

4. How many of these shapes are rectangular prisms?

   Ⓐ 3   Ⓑ 4
   Ⓒ 2   Ⓓ 5

5. Which is shaped like a ○ ?

Ⓐ   Ⓑ

Ⓒ   Ⓓ

6. Which is shaped like a △ ?

Ⓐ   Ⓑ

Ⓒ   Ⓓ

7. A triangle has ___ sides.
  Ⓐ 2
  Ⓑ 3
  Ⓒ 4
  Ⓓ 5

8. A square has ___ sides.
  Ⓐ 5
  Ⓑ 3
  Ⓒ 2
  Ⓓ 4

9. A pentagon has ___ sides.
  Ⓐ 5
  Ⓑ 3
  Ⓒ 6
  Ⓓ 8

10. Which of the following shapes has symmetry?

Ⓐ   Ⓑ

Ⓒ   Ⓓ

11. Which of the following shapes does not have symmetry?

Ⓐ   Ⓑ

Ⓒ   Ⓓ

Name   Date

Problem Solving

Directions: Read each story carefully. Fill in the circle next to the correct answer.

Examples: A. Two birds sat in the tree. Four more birds joined them. How many birds in all?
- Ⓐ 2
- Ⓑ 4
- ● 6
- Ⓓ 8

 Think about each question carefully before you choose your answer.

Practice

1. Six boys were in the class. Ten girls were in the class. How many students were in the class altogether?
   - Ⓐ 4
   - Ⓑ 16
   - Ⓒ 60
   - Ⓓ 3

2. Rob bought 8 pieces of candy at the store. He ate 3 before he got home. How many pieces of candy did Rob have when he got home?
   - Ⓐ 3
   - Ⓑ 11
   - Ⓒ 5
   - Ⓓ 6

3. Allie walks 4 dogs on Tuesday, 5 dogs on Wednesday, and 2 dogs on Thursday. How many dogs does Allie walk altogether?
   - Ⓐ 11
   - Ⓑ 9
   - Ⓒ 7
   - Ⓓ 6

4. I bought a shirt for $12 and a pair of socks for $2. How much money did I spend altogether?
   - Ⓐ $10
   - Ⓑ $24
   - Ⓒ $25
   - Ⓓ $14

Name _____ Date _____

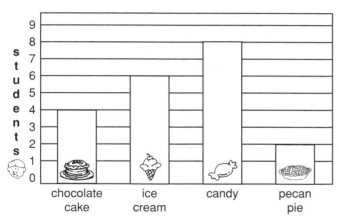

Directions: Use the graph to answer questions 5–8.

5. How many students like ice cream?
   Ⓐ 4
   Ⓑ 6
   Ⓒ 8
   Ⓓ It is not shown on the graph.

6. How many students like brownies?
   Ⓐ 6
   Ⓑ 2
   Ⓒ 8
   Ⓓ It is not shown on the graph.

7. What dessert do the most students like?
   Ⓐ pecan pie
   Ⓑ ice cream
   Ⓒ chocolate cake
   Ⓓ candy

8. What dessert do the fewest students like?
   Ⓐ ice cream
   Ⓑ candy
   Ⓒ chocolate cake
   Ⓓ pecan pie

Directions: Fill in the circle next to the number sentence you would use to solve each word problem.

9. Rachel invited 9 girls and 7 boys to her birthday party. How many children did Rachel invite to her birthday party?
   Ⓐ 9 x 7 = ___
   Ⓑ 9 − 7 = ___
   Ⓒ 9 ÷ 7 = ___
   Ⓓ 9 + 7 = ___

10. Mike can fit seven books on one shelf. How many books can Mike fit on three shelves?
    Ⓐ 7 + 3 = ___
    Ⓑ 7 x 3 = ___
    Ⓒ 7 ÷ 3 = ___
    Ⓓ 7 − 3 = ___

GO ON

Name _____   Date _____

11. Ryan moves five boxes in one hour. How many boxes does Ryan move in two hours?

Ⓐ 2 x 5 = ___
Ⓑ 2 + 5 = ___
Ⓒ 2 − 5 = ___
Ⓓ 2 x 1 = ___

14. Allie ate two more pieces of pie than Lori. Lori ate four pieces of pie. How many pieces of pie did Allie eat?

Ⓐ 2 + 4 = ___
Ⓑ 2 x 4 = ___
Ⓒ 4 − 2 = ___
Ⓓ 4 ÷ 2 = ___

12. Matt had $10. He spent $7 at the movie. How much money did Matt have left over?

Ⓐ 10 + 7 = ___
Ⓑ 10 − 7 = ___
Ⓒ 10 ÷ 7 = ___
Ⓓ 10 x 7 = ___

15. Peter ate 4 pieces of pizza. Nick ate 7 pieces of pizza. How many pieces of pizza did they eat together?

Ⓐ 4 + 7 = ___
Ⓑ 7 − 4 = ___
Ⓒ 7 x 4 = ___
Ⓓ 4 ÷ 7 = ___

13. Hallie ran sixteen miles. Evan ran twelve miles. How many more miles did Hallie run than Evan?

Ⓐ 16 + 12 = ___
Ⓑ 16 x 12 = ___
Ⓒ 16 ÷ 12 = ___
Ⓓ 16 − 12 = ___

16. Jared was sick for 9 days. Sarah was sick for 2 days. How many more days was Jared sick than Sarah?

Ⓐ 9 + 2 = ___
Ⓑ 9 − 2 = ___
Ⓒ 9 ÷ 2 = ___
Ⓓ 9 x 2 = ___

Name _____ Date _____

Sample Test

Directions: Fill in the circle next to the correct answer.

1. Match the times.

   [04:55]

   Ⓐ   Ⓑ
   Ⓒ   Ⓓ

2. Match the times.
   Ⓐ 3:10
   Ⓑ 2:10
   Ⓒ 3:15
   Ⓓ 2:20

3. Kayla starts her homework at 3:30. It takes her 35 minutes to complete her homework. What time does Kayla complete her homework?
   Ⓐ 3:35
   Ⓑ 4:05
   Ⓒ 4:10
   Ⓓ 4:00

4. Grace leaves for the library at a quarter to five. What time does Grace leave for the library?
   Ⓐ 5:15
   Ⓑ 5:30
   Ⓒ 4:45
   Ⓓ 4:30

5. Which clock shows 8:25?
   Ⓐ   Ⓑ
   Ⓒ   Ⓓ

6. Howie has $1. He buys a pencil for 35¢. How much change does Howie get?
   Ⓐ 75¢
   Ⓑ 70¢
   Ⓒ 65¢
   Ⓓ 60¢

GO ON

7. Annie has $5. She wants to buy a notebook that costs $2 and a pen for $1. Does she have enough money?
   Ⓐ yes
   Ⓑ no

8. How much money?

   Ⓐ $1
   Ⓑ 76¢
   Ⓒ 47¢
   Ⓓ 46¢

9. How much money?

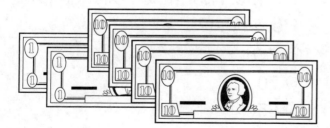

   Ⓐ $24
   Ⓑ $42
   Ⓒ $6
   Ⓓ $16

10. How much money?

    Ⓐ $53.12
    Ⓑ $39.12
    Ⓒ $35.52
    Ⓓ $35.70

11. Choose the best estimate.
    43 + 32 = ___
    Ⓐ 70
    Ⓑ 80
    Ⓒ 85
    Ⓓ 65

12. Choose the best estimate.
    49 + 22 + 13 = ___
    Ⓐ 90
    Ⓑ 70
    Ⓒ 80
    Ⓓ 60

Name _____ Date _____

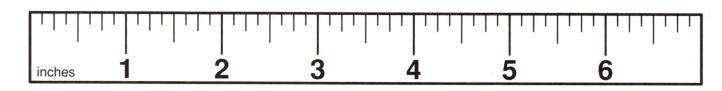

Directions: Use the ruler and the lines to answer questions 13–15.

13. What is the length of the longest line?
   Ⓐ 2 inches   Ⓑ 4 inches
   Ⓒ $3\frac{1}{2}$ inches   Ⓓ 3 inches

14. What is the length of the shortest line?
   Ⓐ 2 inches   Ⓑ $2\frac{1}{2}$ inches
   Ⓒ 3 inches   Ⓓ 1 inch

15. If you added the shortest line to the middle line, how long would your new line be?
   Ⓐ 5 inches   Ⓑ $5\frac{1}{2}$ inches
   Ⓒ 6 inches   Ⓓ 1 inch

16. What fraction of the circle is not shaded?
   Ⓐ $\frac{1}{3}$
   Ⓑ $\frac{2}{3}$
   Ⓒ $\frac{1}{2}$
   Ⓓ $\frac{3}{4}$
   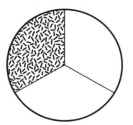

17. What fraction of the pictures are bulbs?

   Ⓐ $\frac{1}{4}$ Ⓑ $\frac{1}{3}$
   Ⓒ $\frac{2}{4}$ Ⓓ $\frac{1}{2}$

GO ON

18. Which shows 1 quart?

Ⓐ   Ⓑ

Ⓒ   Ⓓ

19. Which shows 1 gallon?

Ⓐ   Ⓑ

Ⓒ   Ⓓ

20. Which shows symmetry?

Ⓐ   Ⓑ

Ⓒ   Ⓓ

21. Which is shaped like a sphere?

Ⓐ   Ⓑ

Ⓒ   Ⓓ

22. Marta buys 3 new books at the store. Jackie buys 8 new books. How many more books does Jackie buy than Marta?

Ⓐ 11   Ⓑ 4
Ⓒ 5   Ⓓ 24

23. Tanner spends $2 at the school store. Matt spends $3 at the school store. How much money do Tanner and Matt spend altogether?

Ⓐ $6   Ⓑ $1
Ⓒ $7   Ⓓ $5

24. Joe gets out of school at 3:30. Today he had to leave at 1:30. How many hours of school did he miss?

Ⓐ 1   Ⓑ 2
Ⓒ 6   Ⓓ 3

			July			
Sunday	Monday	Tuesday	Wednesday	Thursday	Friday	Saturday
				1	2	3
4 Independence Day	5	6	7	8	9	10
11	12	13	14 Allie's birthday	15	16	17
18	19	20	21	22	23	24
25	26	27	28	29	30	31

Directions: Use the calendar to answer questions 21–24.

25. What day of the week is Independance Day?

Ⓐ Sunday
Ⓑ Monday
Ⓒ Friday
Ⓓ Thursday

26. What day of the week is July 17?

Ⓐ Monday
Ⓑ Tuesday
Ⓒ Friday
Ⓓ Saturday

27. What is the date of the third Monday in July?

Ⓐ 5
Ⓑ 12
Ⓒ 19
Ⓓ 26

28. Allie is having a birthday party on July 14. If today is July 6, how many more days does she have to wait for her party?

Ⓐ 7
Ⓑ 8
Ⓒ 20
Ⓓ 5

Sample Answer Sheet

Answer Pages

Page 7
1. A
2. C
3. B
4. A

Page 8
5. B
6. A
7. D
8. A
9. A
10. A
11. C
12. C

Page 9
13. D
14. A
15. B
16. C
17. C
18. D
19. A
20. B

Page 10
1. C
2. B
3. C
4. D

Page 11
5. A
6. A
7. A
8. B
9. A
10. A
11. C
12. B
13. A

Page 12
1. B
2. C
3. A
4. C

Page 13
5. B
6. A
7. A
8. C
9. B
10. B
11. A
12. C

Page 14
13. B
14. A
15. C
16. B
17. B
18. A
19. B
20. B

Page 15
1. D
2. A
3. B
4. C

Page 16
5. A
6. C
7. B
8. A
9. C
10. D
11. C
12. A

Page 17
13. B
14. A
15. B
16. B
17. D
18. D
19. A
20. B

Page 18
1. B
2. A
3. A
4. C

Page 19
5. C
6. A
7. B
8. A
9. A
10. A
11. D
12. A

Page 20
1. C
2. A
3. A
4. A
5. A
6. B

Page 21
1. C
2. A
3. C
4. B

Page 22
5. C
6. B
7. A
8. D
9. D
10. A
11. D
12. B

Page 23
1. D
2. D
3. C
4. B

Page 24
5. A
6. A
7. A
8. A
9. A
10. D
11. A
12. B

Page 25
1. C
2. A
3. A
4. C
5. A
6. C
7. C

Page 26
8. C
9. A
10. A
11. C
12. C
13. D

Answer Pages

Page 27
14. B
15. C
16. A
17. B
18. B
19. C
20. A
21. D
22. B
23. A

Page 28
24. B
25. C
26. A
27. C
28. A
29. B
30. D

Page 29
31. C
32. B
33. C
34. D
35. A
36. B
37. D
38. C

Page 30
1. C
2. D
3. C
4. B

Page 31
5. C
6. A
7. B
8. C
9. D
10. A

Page 32
1. A
2. B
3. A
4. B
5. D
6. C

Page 33
7. D
8. A
9. B
10. C
11. B
12. D
13. B
14. C
15. D

Page 34
1. B
2. C
3. D
4. B
5. B
6. C

Page 35
7. D
8. A
9. B
10. B
11. C
12. B
13. C
14. D

Page 36
1. B
2. B
3. B
4. B

Page 37
5. C
6. D
7. A
8. C
9. B
10. B
11. B
12. D
13. A
14. C

Page 38
1. B
2. B
3. A
4. B
5. B
6. B

Page 39
1. C
2. B
3. B
4. A
5. D
6. C

Page 40
1. C
2. B
3. B
4. B

Page 41
5. B
6. A
7. C
8. B
9. A
10. B
11. B
12. A

Page 42
1. B
2. A
3. C
4. D

Page 43
5. C
6. A
7. B
8. C
9. B
10. B
11. B
12. B

Page 44
13. A
14. C
15. B
16. D
17. B
18. A
19. B
20. A

Page 45
21. C
22. A
23. D
24. C
25. B
26. B
27. A
28. B
29. C

Page 46
1. D
2. C
3. B
4. A
5. B

Answer Pages

Page 47
6. A
7. B
8. A
9. C
10. B
11. D
12. C

Page 48
1. C
2. C
3. D
4. C

Page 49
1. C
2. D
3. A
4. B

Page 50
1. A
2. C

Page 51
1. B
2. A
3. C
4. A
5. D
6. A

Page 52
1. A
2. B
3. B
4. C

Page 53
1. A
2. C
3. B
4. D
5. A
6. B

Page 54
7. A
8. C
9. B
10. D
11. C
12. A
13. C
14. D

Page 55
1. B
2. B
3. A
4. A

Page 56
1. B
2. C
3. A
4. C

Page 57
1. C
2. B
3. A
4. A
5. B
6. A
7. B
8. A

Page 58
1. B
2. C
3. C
4. A
5. C
6. C
7. C
8. B

Page 59
9. D
10. B
11. A
12. B
13. C
14. B
15. A

Page 60
1. B
2. C
3. B
4. B
5. C
6. B

Page 61
1. B
2. C
3. A
4. A
5. B
6. B
7. A
8. C

Page 62
1. C
2. C
3. B
4. A
5. B
6. A

Page 63
1. A
2. B
3. A
4. C
5. D
6. A

Page 64
7. B
8. A
9. C
10. B
11. C
12. A

Page 65
13. A
14. B
15. A
16. A
17. D
18. A

Page 66
1. C
2. D
3. A
4. B

Page 67
5. A
6. D
7. A
8. A
9. B
10. A

Page 68
1. B
2. D
3. A
4. A
5. B
6. B
7. D
8. A
9. D
10. A

Answer Pages

Page 69

1. Ⓐ ● Ⓒ
2. ● Ⓑ Ⓒ
3. Ⓐ ● Ⓒ
4. Ⓐ Ⓑ ●
5. ● Ⓑ Ⓒ
6. Ⓐ Ⓑ ●
7. Ⓐ ● Ⓒ
8. ● Ⓑ Ⓒ
9. Ⓐ ● Ⓒ
10. Ⓐ Ⓑ ●

Page 70

1. Ⓐ Ⓑ ●
2. ● Ⓑ Ⓒ
3. Ⓐ ● Ⓒ
4. Ⓐ Ⓑ ●

Page 71

5. Ⓐ Ⓑ ●
6. Ⓐ ● Ⓒ
7. Ⓐ ● Ⓒ
8. ● Ⓑ Ⓒ
9. ● Ⓑ Ⓒ
10. Ⓐ Ⓑ ●

Page 72

1. Ⓐ ● Ⓒ Ⓓ
2. ● Ⓑ Ⓒ Ⓓ
3. Ⓐ Ⓑ ● Ⓓ
4. Ⓐ ● Ⓒ Ⓓ
5. ● Ⓑ Ⓒ Ⓓ
6. ● Ⓑ Ⓒ Ⓓ
7. Ⓐ ● Ⓒ Ⓓ
8. Ⓐ Ⓑ Ⓒ ●
9. ● Ⓑ Ⓒ Ⓓ

Page 73

10. Ⓐ Ⓑ Ⓒ ●
11. Ⓐ Ⓑ Ⓒ ●
12. Ⓐ ● Ⓒ
13. ● Ⓑ Ⓒ
14. Ⓐ ● Ⓒ
15. ● Ⓑ Ⓒ
16. Ⓐ ● Ⓒ
17. Ⓐ Ⓑ ●

Page 74

18. Ⓐ Ⓑ ● Ⓓ
19. ● Ⓑ Ⓒ Ⓓ
20. Ⓐ Ⓑ ● Ⓓ
21. Ⓐ ● Ⓒ Ⓓ
22. Ⓐ ● Ⓒ
23. Ⓐ Ⓑ ●
24. ● Ⓑ Ⓒ

Page 75

25. ● Ⓑ Ⓒ
26. Ⓐ ● Ⓒ
27. ● Ⓑ Ⓒ
28. Ⓐ Ⓑ ●
29. ● Ⓑ Ⓒ
30. Ⓐ Ⓑ ●
31. Ⓐ ● Ⓒ
32. Ⓐ Ⓑ ●
33. ● Ⓑ Ⓒ

Page 76

1. Ⓐ Ⓑ ● Ⓓ
2. Ⓐ Ⓑ Ⓒ ●
3. Ⓐ ● Ⓒ Ⓓ
4. Ⓐ Ⓑ Ⓒ ●
5. ● Ⓑ Ⓒ Ⓓ
6. ● Ⓑ Ⓒ Ⓓ

Page 77

7. ● Ⓑ Ⓒ Ⓓ
8. Ⓐ Ⓑ Ⓒ ●
9. Ⓐ ● Ⓒ Ⓓ
10. Ⓐ ● Ⓒ Ⓓ
11. ● Ⓑ Ⓒ Ⓓ
12. Ⓐ Ⓑ ● Ⓓ
13. Ⓐ Ⓑ Ⓒ ●
14. Ⓐ ● Ⓒ Ⓓ

Page 78

1. Ⓐ ● Ⓒ
2. Ⓐ ● Ⓒ
3. ● Ⓑ Ⓒ
4. Ⓐ ● Ⓒ
5. ● Ⓑ Ⓒ
6. Ⓐ Ⓑ ●

Page 79

7. Ⓐ ● Ⓒ
8. Ⓐ Ⓑ ●
9. Ⓐ Ⓑ ●
10. Ⓐ ● Ⓒ
11. Ⓐ ● Ⓒ
12. ● Ⓑ Ⓒ
13. ● Ⓑ Ⓒ
14. Ⓐ ● Ⓒ
15. ● Ⓑ Ⓒ
16. ● Ⓑ Ⓒ

Page 80

1. Ⓐ ● Ⓒ Ⓓ
2. ● Ⓑ Ⓒ Ⓓ
3. Ⓐ ● Ⓒ Ⓓ
4. Ⓐ Ⓑ ● Ⓓ

Page 81

5. Ⓐ ● Ⓒ Ⓓ
6. Ⓐ Ⓑ ● Ⓓ
7. ● Ⓑ Ⓒ Ⓓ
8. Ⓐ ● Ⓒ Ⓓ
9. Ⓐ Ⓑ ● Ⓓ
10. Ⓐ Ⓑ Ⓒ ●
11. Ⓐ ● Ⓒ Ⓓ
12. Ⓐ Ⓑ ● Ⓓ

Page 82

13. Ⓐ ● Ⓒ Ⓓ
14. Ⓐ Ⓑ ● Ⓓ
15. Ⓐ Ⓑ Ⓒ ●
16. Ⓐ ● Ⓒ Ⓓ
17. ● Ⓑ Ⓒ Ⓓ
18. Ⓐ ● Ⓒ Ⓓ
19. ● Ⓑ Ⓒ Ⓓ
20. Ⓐ Ⓑ ● Ⓓ

Page 83

21. Ⓐ Ⓑ ●
22. ● Ⓑ Ⓒ
23. ● Ⓑ Ⓒ
24. Ⓐ Ⓑ ●
25. ● Ⓑ Ⓒ
26. Ⓐ Ⓑ ●
27. ● Ⓑ Ⓒ
28. Ⓐ Ⓑ ●
29. ● Ⓑ Ⓒ
30. ● Ⓑ Ⓒ

Page 84

1. Ⓐ ● Ⓒ Ⓓ
2. ● Ⓑ Ⓒ Ⓓ
3. Ⓐ ● Ⓒ Ⓓ

Page 85

4. Ⓐ ● Ⓒ Ⓓ
5. ● Ⓑ Ⓒ Ⓓ
6. Ⓐ Ⓑ ● Ⓓ
7. Ⓐ Ⓑ Ⓒ ●
8. Ⓐ Ⓑ ● Ⓓ
9. ● Ⓑ Ⓒ Ⓓ

Page 86

10. ● Ⓑ
11. Ⓐ ●
12. ● Ⓑ
13. Ⓐ ●
14. ● Ⓑ
15. Ⓐ ●
16. Ⓐ ●
17. Ⓐ ●

Page 87

18. Ⓐ Ⓑ ●
19. Ⓐ ● Ⓒ
20. Ⓐ ● Ⓒ
21. ● Ⓑ Ⓒ

Answer Pages

Page 88
22. B
23. B
24. B
25. C
26. B
27. C
28. A

Page 89
1. B
2. C
3. B
4. C
5. C
6. B

Page 90
7. A
8. B
9. A
10. C
11. B
12. B

Page 91
13. B
14. B
15. A
16. B
17. A

Page 92
18. A
19. C
20. C
21. A

Page 93
1. B
2. A
3. D
4. B
5. C
6. A

7. B
8. C

Page 94
9. C
10. B
11. B
12. A
13. A
14. D
15. C
16. A
17. C

Page 95
18. A
19. C
20. B
21. A
22. A
23. A

Page 96
24. C
25. A
24. B
24. B

Page 97
1. A
2. A
3. C
4. D
5. B
6. A

Page 98
7. B
8. A
9. C
10. A
11. C
12. A
13. A
14. C

Page 99
15. B
16. A
17. B
18. A
19. C
20. B

Page 100
1. B
2. A
3. B
4. A
5. B
6. D

Page 101
7. B
8. A
9. A
10. B

Page 102
1. D
2. C
3. B
4. A

Page 103
5. C
6. D
7. B
8. A
9. A
10. D

Page 104
11. B
12. C
13. B
14. B
15. A
16. B

Page 105
17. B
18. C
19. D
20. A
21. D
22. A

Page 106
1. A
2. D
3. D
4. D
5. A
6. C

Page 107
7. D
8. C
9. A
10. A
11. D
12. A

Page 108
13. B
14. A
15. B
16. A

Page 109
1. C
2. B
3. B
4. D
5. C
6. B
7. A

Answer Pages

Page 110
8. C
9. A
10. D
11. C
12. B
13. B

Page 111
14. A
15. C
16. A
17. B
18. C
19. A
20. A

Page 112
1. B
2. A
3. D
4. C
5. B
6. A

Page 113
7. B
8. D
9. C
10. B
11. A
12. D
13. C
14. B

Page 114
15. D
16. A
17. B
18. C
19. B
20. B
21. C
22. D

Page 115
1. B
2. A
3. D
4. C
5. B
6. C

Page 116
7. A
8. C
9. D
10. B
11. C
12. C
13. D
14. A

Page 117
15. B
16. C
17. C
18. D
19. A
20. C
21. C
22. C

Page 118
1. B
2. D
3. C
4. C
5. A
6. C

Page 119
7. B
8. C
9. A
10. D
11. C
12. C
13. C
14. B

Page 120
15. B
16. C
17. C
18. D
19. C
20. C
21. B
22. D

Page 121
1. B
2. C
3. A
4. B

Page 122
5. A
6. D
7. B
8. C
9. C
10. C
11. C
12. B

Page 123
1. D
2. A
3. C
4. A
5. A
6. D

Page 124
1. B
2. C
3. D
4. C
5. A
6. A
7. C
8. D

Page 125
9. D
10. B
11. A
12. D
13. A
14. C
15. C
16. C

Page 126
17. B
18. C
19. C
20. C
21. C
22. C
23. D
24. C

Page 127
25. B
26. A
27. C
28. D
29. C
30. A
31. D
32. A

Page 128
1. A
2. C
3. D
4. C

Page 129
5. B
6. A
7. B
8. C
9. C
10. C

Answer Pages

Page 130
11. C
12. A
13. D
14. B
15. B
16. C
17. D

Page 131
18. B
19. C
20. D
21. B
22. B

Page 132
1. C
2. B
3. A
4. A
5. B
6. C

Page 133
7. B
8. C
9. A
10. B
11. D
12. C

Page 134
13. C
14. D
15. A
16. D

Page 135
1. D
2. B
3. B
4. C
5. C
6. A

Page 136
7. D
8. B
9. D
10. B
11. D
12. D
13. B
14. A

Page 137
15. D
16. B
17. B
18. B
19. B
20. D
21. C
22. B

Page 138
1. B
2. C
3. C
4. D

Page 139
5. A
6. B
7. C
8. D
9. C
10. A

Page 140
1. A
2. D

Page 141
3. C
4. B
5. A
6. D
7. D
8. B

Page 142
1. A
2. D
3. B
4. C

Page 143
5. D
6. B
7. B
8. B
9. A
10. A
11. D

Page 144
1. B
2. C
3. B
4. D

Page 145
5. B
6. D
7. D
8. D
9. B
10. B

Page 146
11. A
12. B
13. D
14. B
15. B
16. B

Page 147
1. A
2. C
3. B
4. C
5. C
6. C

Page 148
7. B
8. D
9. B
10. B
11. A
12. C

Page 149
13. B
14. B
15. B
16. A
17. A

Page 150
18. B
19. C
20. B
21. B
22. C
23. D
24. B

Page 151
25. A
26. D
27. C
28. B